JUSTICE IN COLONIAL VIRGINIA

Da Capo Press Reprints in

AMERICAN CONSTITUTIONAL AND LEGAL HISTORY

GENERAL EDITOR: LEONARD W. LEVY
Claremont Graduate School

JUSTICE IN
COLONIAL VIRGINIA

By Oliver P. Chitwood, *erry* *1874 -*

DA CAPO PRESS · NEW YORK · 1971

A Da Capo Press Reprint Edition

This Da Capo Press edition of *Justice in Colonial Virginia* is an unabridged republication of the first edition published in Baltimore, Maryland, in 1905 as Series XXIII, Numbers 7-8, in the *Johns Hopkins University Studies in Historical and Political Science.*

Library of Congress Catalog Card Number 72-87557

SBN 306-71388-8

Published by Da Capo Press
A Division of Plenum Publishing Corporation
227 West 17th Street, New York, N.Y. 10011
All Rights Reserved

Manufactured in the United States of America

JUSTICE IN COLONIAL VIRGINIA

SERIES XXIII   Nos. 7-8

JOHNS HOPKINS UNIVERSITY STUDIES

IN

HISTORICAL AND POLITICAL SCIENCE

(Edited by H. B. Adams, 1882-1901)

J. M. VINCENT

J. H. HOLLANDER   W. W. WILLOUGHBY

Editors

———

JUSTICE IN COLONIAL VIRGINIA

BY

OLIVER PERRY CHITWOOD

———

BALTIMORE
THE JOHNS HOPKINS PRESS
PUBLISHED MONTHLY
July-August, 1905

The Lord Baltimore Press
THE FRIEDENWALD COMPANY
BALTIMORE, MD.

CONTENTS

6 *Contents.*

PREFACE

Considerable attention has been devoted to the study of executive and legislative institutions in the American colonies, but so far the judicial institutions have been comparatively neglected. It is for this reason that this inquiry into the origin, history, and growth of the Virginia colonial judiciary has been undertaken. The purpose of this monograph is to describe the judicial machinery, give the stages of evolution through which it has passed, and show the character of the justice administered by the courts. Some attention is also devoted to the part played by the judiciary in the history of the colony. The aim is to present such facts as will be of value to the historian rather than those that will be of interest to the lawyer. Therefore, a detailed account of legal procedure is not attempted.

I wish gratefully to acknowledge my obligations to Dr. J. C. Ballagh, of Johns Hopkins University, at whose suggestion this work was undertaken, and whose advice and criticism have been of great value in its preparation. My thanks are also due to Professors J. M. Vincent, W. W. Willoughby, and B. C. Steiner, of Johns Hopkins University, and J. A. C. Chandler, of Richmond College, who have made valuable suggestions and corrections; and to Mr. W. G. Stanard, of the Virginia Historical Society, whose advice was very helpful to me in the use of the historical sources that are in the libraries of Richmond, Virginia.

JUSTICE IN COLONIAL VIRGINIA

INTRODUCTION.

Preliminary Steps in the Organization of the Judiciary (1607-1619).

When Virginia was settled, English institutions came with the settlers; but these institutions had, in many cases, to undergo changes before they were prepared to enter the new environment into which they were carried by colonization. They had to return to their infancy and in some instances to pass through stages of growth in the new world similar to those through which they had already gone in the old. This second evolution was more rapid than the first; and America in one century reached a stage in institutional progress which it had taken Europe more than a millennium to attain. Only those parts of the old constitution that were suited to the new conditions survived and became a permanent part of the colonial system of government. For the first decade of its existence, Virginia's constitution, therefore, presented few points of similarity to its great prototype, and, in fact, it was not until 1619 that the likeness of the colonial government to that of the mother country became plainly discernible.

The constitutional history of Virginia begins on April 10, 1606, when King James I. granted to the Virginia Company letters-patent for the establishment of two colonies in America. By this charter, the local government of the southern colony was to be entrusted to a resident council composed of thirteen members.[1] In accordance with the instructions given by the King to the Company, the general council in England (which was to exercise a supervising control over both

---

[1] Stith, History of Virginia, Appendix, 3.

the southern and northern colonies) appointed seven men to
be of the Council of Virginia. Their names were put in a
sealed box, which was not opened until April 26, 1607, after
their arrival at Cape Henry.[2]

The local council was to govern the colony according to
the laws of England, and was not allowed to pass ordinances
affecting life or limb. But with the exception of these two
restrictions, its powers were almost absolute. In this
council were vested all the functions of government, legislative, judicial, and executive. The opinion of the majority
was to prevail in all decisions, and the president could cast
two votes in case of a tie. The council was a self-perpetuating body; it had power to fill vacancies and remove
members for just cause, and also to elect its president, who
was to be chosen annually. The crown reserved to itself the
power to punish all persons living in the colony who should
at any time "rob or spoil, by sea or land, or do any act
of unjust and unlawful hostility" to the citizens of friendly
states.

But the council, acting in its judicial capacity, was to try all
other offenders, except those who should attempt to seduce
any of the colonists from their allegiance to the King and
the established religion. Such of these as could not be
brought to repentance by imprisonment were to be sent to
England for trial. By the instructions given by the King, certain offenses, as "tumults, rebellion, conspiracies, mutiny,
and seditions in those parts which may be dangerous to the
states there, together with murther, manslaughter, incest,
rapes, and adulteries," were made punishable by death, and
except for manslaughter, the benefit of clergy was not to be
allowed for any of them. In every arraignment for these

---

[2] Neill, Virginia Company, 5-6. Brown, Genesis of the United
States, 56, 57. Purchas, His Pilgrimmes, IV, 1705. The members
of the first council were Bartholomew Gosnold, Edward Maria
Wingfield, Christopher Newport, John Smith, John Martin, John
Ratcliffe, and George Kendall. Why thirteen were not appointed, in
accordance with the provisions of the charter, does not appear from
the documents.

crimes, the accused was to be tried by a jury of twelve men unless he confessed his crime or stood mute, in which case judgment was to be passed by the president and council, or " the major part thereof." For minor breaches of its ordinances, the council, by a majority vote, could, without calling in a jury, inflict such penalties as fines, imprisonment, and reasonable corporal punishment. The judicial proceedings were to be conducted orally ; but a record was to be made of all cases decided by the court. Persons convicted of capital charges could be reprieved by the council, but only by the King could they be pardoned.[3]

Thus the government of Virginia began as an oligarchy. Gosnold wielded a great influence in the council, and as long as he lived affairs in the colony moved on with comparative smoothness. But after his death the spirit of strife, no longer controlled by his commanding presence, broke out among the rulers, and Wingfield and Kendall were deposed.[4] The majority of the council were not unmindful of their power to expel offending members from their body, but did not show an equal willingness to comply with that part of their instructions which required them to fill vacancies. Consequently, after the expulsion of Kendall and Wingfield, Newport having returned to England, the number of councillors was reduced to three, Ratcliffe being president.

Inimical relations continued to exist between the councillors, and dissentions never ceased to rise until another form of government had been adopted by the colony. Several other members were added to the council, but, by the spring of 1609, the number had been so reduced by deaths and removals that Smith was left sole councillor.[5]

During the period of Ratcliffe's presidency, judicial deci-

---

[3] Brown, Genesis of the United States, 67-71, 73, 74; Wingfield, Discourse in Arber, Works of Captain John Smith, p. LXXX.
[4] Percy's Discourse, published in Brown's Gen., 167, 168; Wingfield's Discourse, published in Arber's Smith, LXXVI, 95.
[5] Arber, Works of Smith, 95, 404, 432, 435, 466.

sions were not characterized by the fairness becoming a
tribunal of justice. Private spite influenced the councillors
to pass unjust sentence against those who had incurred their
dislike.⁶ However, during Smith's administration, justice
seems to have been evenly meted out to all. Offenders were
punished, but not undeservedly. Some of the penalties that
Smith inflicted for the correction of evil-doers were whipping and " laying by the heels." He made threats of hanging, sent some offenders to England, and ordered certain
men to slay the treacherous Dutchmen who were plotting
against his life with the Powhatan. As a remedy for the
sin of swearing, he employed the water cure in a unique
way.⁷

A very important change was made in the government of
the colony by the second charter, which was granted to the
Company in 1609. A governor was appointed by the Company to supersede the local council and was given almost
absolute power in the government of the colony.⁸ Lord De
La Warr, who was chosen for this responsible place, did not
go to Virginia until next year; but in the meantime Sir
Thomas Gates had been sent over with a commission to act as
governor. He was shipwrecked off the coast of the
Bermudas and detained on those islands for nine months,
and, therefore, did not reach Virginia until the spring of

---

⁶ A blacksmith by the name of Reade was sentenced to death for
" giving bad language" to President Ratcliffe and threatening to
strike him with some of his tools. Reade bought his pardon by be-
traying a conspiracy headed by Kendall, who was tried and shot.
  When Smith returned from his Indian captivity, some of his enemies united with Ratcliffe in an attempt to have him put to death.
They charged him with complicity in the murder of his two companions, who had been killed by the Indians, and claimed that according to the Mosiac law he was responsible for their death. But
Captain Newport arrived from England just at this time and kept
them from carrying out their murderous designs. Arber, Works of
Smith, 12, 13, 22, 23, 401.
  ⁷ Every oath that the men uttered during the day was registered,
and at night a can of cold water for each was poured down the
sleeve of the blasphemer to wash away his sin. Arber, Works of
Smith, 126, 168, 169, 401, 473, 480, 481, 483.
  ⁸ Brown, Genesis of the United States, 208, 233, 234, 375-380.

1610, just in time to drop the curtain on the closing scene of the " Starving Time." The council, into whose hands the reins of government had fallen on Smith's departure, now surrendered their authority to Gates, the lieutenant-governor. Prior to this time, a few provisions in the King's instructions were the only rules that had been given to the councillors to guide them in the performance of their judicial duties. But Gates now initiated a system of justice by which judicial decisions were to be rendered in accordance with laws made to suit the peculiar conditions that then obtained in the colony. He wrote out certain rules and ordinances by which the settlers were to be governed during his short rule in the colony and posted them in the church at Jamestown. He thus proclaimed the first legal code ever put in practice in English-speaking America.[9]

In June, Gates was superseded by Lord De La Warr, who, on his arrival in Virginia, selected six men to constitute his council. They were to act only as an advisory body, and did not in any way limit his authority. He had power to remove any of them whenever he saw cause for so doing. Just what part the council played in the administration of justice for the next nine years cannot be determined ; but it may be safely inferred from Lord De La Warr's commission and other documents, that during this period the councillors acted only as advisors to the governor in the trial of causes.[10]

The laws proclaimed by Gates were " approved and exemplified " by Lord De La Warr. They were afterwards enlarged by Sir Thomas Dale by the addition of certain articles taken from the martial code of Holland. In this amended form they were sent to Sir Thomas Smith, the Treasurer of the Company, who approved of them and had

---

[9] Strachey, A True Repertory of the Wracke and Redemption of Sir Thomas Gates, Knight, printed by Purchas, 1748-1749.
[10] Strachey, A True Repertory, etc., printed in Purchas, IV, 1754. Brown, Genesis of the United States, 380. Proceedings of the Virginia Company, I, 187. Neill's Va. Company, 42, 43.

them printed for the use of the colony.[11]   From 1611 until
1619, the colony was governed according to these stern and
cruel laws (though the severity of them was afterward
toned down considerably), which were known as "Articles,
Lawes and Orders, Divine, Politique, Martiall." These
laws (which Dale perhaps considered divine in their purpose) made stealing grapes or ears of corn from the public
or private gardens an offense punishable by death. Soldiers
who should cowardly run away from battle without attempt-
ing to fight, and all persons giving to masters of ships com-
modities to be taken out of the country for their own private
use, were to receive the death penalty.   Blasphemy, for the
second offense, was to be punished by having the offending
tongue thrust through with a bodkin.   Absence for the
third time from any one of the two Sunday church services
was a capital crime.   Some other punishments mentioned
were whipping, cutting off ears, and tying neck and heels
together.   Sometimes the unfortunate culprit had to lie in
this position for forty-eight hours.   Any one who violated
a certain article of these laws had to lie feet and head together every night for a month.

The colony being under martial law, the captains and
lieutenants had the power to punish the soldiers of their
companies for certain misdeeds.   The officers subordinate
to them reported disorders to their superiors, and in their
absence punished minor offenses.   But the most important
cases, both civil and military, were referred to the court
martial for trial.   In this tribunal sat the captains of the
companies, and when any of them were absent, their places
in the court were filled by their lieutenants.   Offenders who
were to be arraigned for trial were kept in the custody of
the provost marshal.[12]

It is difficult to say how much severity Dale and his suc-

---

[11] Proceedings of Virginia Company, II, 187. Colonial Records
of Va., 74.
[12] Articles, Lawes, and Orders, Divine, etc., printed in Force's
Tracts, Vol. III, 10, 14, 16-18, 21-26, 38, 40, 46-48, 52, 56.   Works
of John Smith, ed. by Arber, 507, 508.

cessors put into their execution of these laws. If we are to trust entirely an account of their rule which was given by the party of opposition in Virginia in a memorial sent to England in 1624, we cannot but believe that the rigor of these laws was increased rather than diminished in the execution. According to the statement of the "ancient planters"—as the authors of this document styled themselves—the colonists were kept in a state of "slavery" by their rulers. Cruel and inhuman punishments were inflicted without trial by jury and sometimes for trivial offenses. Among the penalties to which the settlers were subjected, they mentioned hanging, burning, and breaking on the wheel. Some of the colonists were hanged for "stealing to satisfy their hunger." One case is given in which a law-breaker "had a bodkin thrust through his tongue and was chained to a tree until he perished." Many of the settlers, they said, found the government intolerable; some of them committed suicide, while others hid themselves away in holes dug in the ground in order to escape its horrors.[13]

However, it would not be just to Dale and the court party in the Company to accept without question this severe indictment brought against their colonial policy by their enemies. Sir Thomas Smith said that some of these laws were promulgated with no intention of being carried out, but only for the purpose of terrorizing the settlers into obedience to the government regulations.

Furthermore, the Rev. Alexander Whittaker, one of the ministers who lived in the colony during this period, did not consider that Dale's rule was unjustly harsh. In speaking of it, he said: "I marvel much that any men of honest life should fear the sword of the magistrate which is unsheathed only in their defence."[14] Another prominent settler, Ralph Hamor, declared that such severity as that practiced by

---

[13] Colonial Records of Virginia 74 et seq. Stith, History of Va., 305.
[14] Purchas, IV, 1771.

Dale was at that time necessary to keep the colony from ruin.[15]

We must also not forget that many of the settlers that Dale and his successors had to deal with were a class of men who would not work except when driven to it by the taskmaster. This was proved by the fact that when the pressure on them was somewhat relieved they relapsed into habits of idleness. When Dale first came to Virginia shortly after Lord De La Warr's departure, he found the colonists playing at bowls in the streets of Jamestown to the utter neglect of their crops.[16] So we see that the ills of the colony were such as could not be remedied except by heroic treatment. But even after discounting fully the *ex parte* evidence against Dale and his successors and making due allowance for the character of the settlers under their control, we are bound to admit that they erred greatly on the side of severity in subjecting the settlers to such a merciless system of government.

The first twelve years of the colony's history was a period of discipline and suspension of constitutional rights. This abridgment of the personal rights of the colonists was due partly to the character of the settlers and the difficulties which a parent state always encounters in founding distant colonies, and partly to the mistaken policy of the faction controlling the London Company. But by 1619, when Yeardley became governor,[17] the colony was established on so firm a basis that the need for military rule ceased, and the Virginians began to enjoy the rights of other Englishmen. When, however, the old military tyranny gave place to the new regime, after the victory of the Sandys party in the government of the Company, some of the old governmental machinery remained to be employed by Yeardley and his successors. Thus we find that the provost marshal con-

---

[15] Smith's Works (Arber ed.), 508.

[16] Smith's Works, 507.

[17] Yeardley was commissioned governor in 1618, but he did not arrive in Virginia until the spring of 1619. Hening, I, 3. Colonial Records of Virgnia, 81.

tinued for some time to perform a part at least of his old duties, and that the commander of the hundred was, in his judicial capacity, transferred from the court martial to the monthly court.[18]

In 1619, the Virginia constitution began to crystallize into its permanent form. Soon the executive, legislative and judicial functions of the government began to be distinguished and assigned to three departments, though the separation in the beginning was only partial and never approached completeness during the entire colonial period. The institutional growth of the colony had not gone far before three channels of administration were found for justice, the assembly, the Quarter Court, and the monthly courts. For a good many years, these were the only courts of justice in Virginia.

The assembly was the supreme court in the colony until about 1682, at which time it was deprived of its authority to try appeals. Its jurisdiction was both original and appellate and extended to both civil and criminal causes. Next to the assembly in the order of jurisdiction came the Quarter or General Court, which was composed of the governor and his council. It, too, had jurisdiction in both civil and criminal cases; but, as a rule, the causes of which it took cognizance were more important than those that were usually determined by the lower courts. It was the most important criminal court in Virginia, and for about three decades after appeals to the assembly were discontinued, it was the only regular tribunal that could try freemen charged with offenses punishable by loss of life or member. In the first quarter of the eighteenth century, a regular court of oyer and terminer was established, and from that time until the Revolution it shared with the General Court the authority to try the more important criminal offenses. These were the only superior courts in the colony. The monthly or

---

[18] Colonial Records of Virgnia, 20. Accomac County Court Records, 1632-40, 10, 20. Robinson MS., 58. Hening, Statutes at Large, I, 125. See pp. 75-108.

county court was the most important inferior court, and during the greater part of the seventeenth century it was the only one in Virginia. The first monthly courts were organized as early as 1624; and when the colony was divided into shires, a separate court was appointed for each. In 1643, the name *county court* was substituted for that of *monthly court.* In 1662, circuit courts were established, which were to try appeals from the county courts. But these courts were expensive, and for this reason were abolished by an act of assembly passed in December of this same year. Out of the county court there had developed in each county, probably by the end of the seventeenth century, and certainly by the beginning of the eighteenth century (1705), a special court for the examination of criminals charged with grave offenses. In 1692, provision was made for the organization in each county of a special court for the trial of slaves accused of capital crimes. Two courts of Hustings were established in the first half of the eighteenth century, one at Williamsburg in 1722, and the other at Norfolk in 1736. Courts martial were held once a year or oftener in each county, by which militiamen were tried for delinquencies and insubordination at musters. These were the inferior courts. Appeals were allowed from the inferior courts to the General Court and from it to the assembly. Appeals were also allowed to England, even from a very early period. In addition to the courts already mentioned, there was a court of Vice-Admiralty, which was established in 1698, and the Court of the Commissary of the Bishop of London. Strictly speaking, the last two should not be classed either with the superior or inferior courts; but for the sake of convenience, they are treated in the chapter on superior courts.

These classes of courts will now be treated in the order of their jurisdiction.

CHAPTER I.

JUDICIAL POWERS OF THE ASSEMBLY.

On July 30th, 1619, there assembled in the church at Jamestown the first representative legislative body that ever convened in English America. This assembly was composed of two representatives from each of the eleven [1] plantations in the colony, who had been chosen in obedience to an order of Governor Yeardley. The governor, sitting in the midst of his council, who were ranged on his right and left, welcomed the Burgesses, as the deputies were called, in the choir of the church. After the opening prayer, the Burgesses went to the body of the church, and the meeting entered upon its work. The assembly thus organized developed into a bicameral legislature like the English Parliament, the governor and council were the upper house, and the Burgesses, corresponding to the Commons in England, constituted the lower house. [2]

Though the duties of the assembly were mainly legislative, yet from the beginning until the latter part of the seventeenth century, it also acted as a court of justice, being the highest judicial tribunal in the colony. It was not, however, the intention of the legislature to compete with the courts for an equal share in the administration of justice. Even at their first session, the Burgesses, by referring two cases to the governor and council for trial, showed a disposition to leave the settling of disputes to a tribunal better

---

[1] The two delegates representing Captain Martin's plantation were not allowed to take their seats because Captain Martin would not surrender the rights of his patent, by which it seems that he was freed from the authority of the Virginia government. This left only twenty representatives, and in a few days one of the deputies died, which reduced the number to nineteen. Colonial Records of Virginia, 9-12, 18, 20 et seq.

[2] Hartwell, Blair, and Chilton, 32.

qualified to decide suits than a parliamentary body.[3] They
must have realized that they could not weigh evidence so
carefully or mete out justice so evenly as a smaller court
composed of experienced judges. Besides, as the country
developed, the legislative demands on the assembly grew
apace, and left it less and less time for other business.
Then, too, as the court system grew in efficiency, the need
for calling on the legislature to decide causes correspond-
ingly diminished.[4]

The assembly was the fountain head of justice, and exercised a supervisory control over the courts. By a statute
of 1662, the first day of every session of the assembly was
to be set aside for hearing indictments made by grand juries
and for inquiring into the methods employed by the courts
and abuses practiced by judges and juries.[5] The legislature
never conceded to the judiciary the right to pass upon the
constitutionality of any of its laws, but plainly declared by
enactments made at different times that no order of court
should contravene an act of assembly.[6]

The assembly, like the Parliament of England, had authority to pass bills of attainder against notorious offenders,
and this privilege was not abrogated by the King's order
which deprived it of its authority to try appeals. But this
power was not the source of any great and lasting injustice
to the people, as it was very rarely called into use. Only two
instances have been found in which bills of attainder were
passed. The assembly that convened in February, 1677,
immediately after Bacon's Rebellion, declared Nathaniel
Bacon and certain of his followers to be guilty of treason
and ordered their goods to be forfeited to the crown. This
act of attainder was in large measure reversed in June, 1680,
when a bill of pardon covering the offenses of most of those

---

[3] Colonial Records of Virginia, 24, 25.
[4] Hartwell, Blair, and Chilton, Present State of Virginia, 25, 26.
Sainsbury MSS., 1679-1682, 151.
[5] Hening, Statutes at Large, II, 108.
[6] Ibid., I, 264, 447; II, 108.

included in the first act was brought over by Governor Culpeper and unanimously agreed to by the assembly.[7] In 1701 the occasion for another act of attainder arose, the victim this time being, not a political offender, but an outlying slave. A certain negro had for several years been "lying out and lurking in obscure places," during which time he had been destroying crops, robbing houses and committing other injuries to the people. To put a stop to these annoyances, the assembly voted a sentence of death against him and offered a reward of one thousand pounds to any one who would apprehend or kill him.[8]

The jurisdiction of the assembly was, for some years at least, both original and appellate and extended to both civil and criminal cases. From certain statutes enacted in the latter part of the Commonwealth period, we learn that its criminal jurisdiction at that time was concurrent with that of the Quarter Court. Criminal causes which were punishable by loss of life or member were tried in the assembly, or Quarter Court, whichever should first convene after the offender had been apprehended.[9] Just how long criminal causes were determined originally by the assembly does not appear from the records. Its civil jurisdiction was, as early as 1641, limited mainly to appellate cases, as is shown by an order of the Quarter Court made in that year. At that time many petty suits were coming before the legislature to the exclusion of more important business. In

---

[7] Another act of 1677 prescribed penalties to be inflicted on those that had played a minor part in the rebellion. Some of these were ordered to appear before the governor and council and afterwards before their respective county courts and there to acknowledge their fault with ropes around their necks. The justices of Rappahannock seem to have been unwilling to subject the offenders of their county to such a degradation and allowed certain ones to appear in court with tape-lines, instead of ropes, about their necks. This failure to execute properly the orders of the assembly was deemed an act of contempt too flagrant to be passed over unnoticed, and so the General Court ordered the offending magistrates to appear before the assembly to answer for this high contempt of its authority. Hening, Statutes at Large, II, 370-380, 458-464, 557.
[8] Hening, Statutes at Large, III, 210.
[9] Ibid., I, 398, 476.

order to relieve this state of congestion, the governor and council issued a proclamation declaring that for the future no private causes " should be admitted to the court [assembly] except such as are at this [Quarter] court referred to a fixed day or such as should [shall] concern as a party some member of this grand assembly." [10]   While it is probable that the judicial activity of the assembly in civil cases was from this time on generally limited to the determination of causes coming up by appeal from the Quarter Court, still its doors were not completely closed against all other suits. A few years later a law was passed which recognized the right of the county commissioners to refer to the assembly any case in which there was no known law or precedent to guide them in their decisions.   Besides, there was to be admitted to the assembly for trial any cause that had had a hearing in any court, provided an act of injustice had been committed by the award of the lower tribunal.[11]

For some years there were no minimum restrictions on appeals with respect to the amount involved, and the most trivial suits could be brought before the Quarter Court or the assembly for trial.   But these bodies did not mean to consume the greater part of their time in considering unimportant causes, and so threw very effective barriers against the stream of judicial business which would otherwise have flowed into them.   These obstructions took the form of heavy damages to be paid by the appellant when the higher court affirmed the decision of the lower one.   By a statute of 1643, which confirmed a law made the previous year, it was ordered that appellants from the Quarter Court to the assembly should pay treble damages when cast in their suits. But these regulations made the way to the Supreme Court too narrow, and it was deemed expedient, some years later, to lighten the burdens borne by appeals to the assembly, and

---

[10] Robinson MS., 236.

[11] Hening, Statutes at Large, I, 272, 304, 345, 375, 519; ibid., II 65.   Robinson MS., 235.   Virginia Magazine of History and Biography, VIII, 395.   Records of General Court, 1670-1676, 76, 166, 183, 189, 191.

the damages attached to them were reduced to fifty per cent of the original award of the court.[12]

It was not until near the end of the Commonwealth period that an attempt was made to limit appeals from the Quarter Court to the assembly so as to exclude causes in which small amounts were involved. The heavy damages with which appeals were weighted did not prevent " many litigous suites of inconsiderable valewes " from leaving the Quarter Court and going into the assembly. In this way other important business was crowded out of the legislature " to the hindrance of publique affairs." The assembly, therefore (1659), deemed it necessary to limit appeals to it from the governor and council to suits in which the amounts in controversy exceeded 2500 pounds of tobacco. But this discrimination against suits of minor importance proved inconvenient, and next year it was enacted that appeals should thereafter be allowed in all cases from the county courts (the court of Northampton excepted) to the Quarter Court and from there to the assembly.[13]

The assembly transacted its judicial business through a committee of justice composed of members of both houses of the legislature. Causes that were brought before the assembly for trial were referred to this committee, which investigated them and decided what action should be taken regarding them. The decisions of the committee were not binding until they had been confirmed by the whole assembly. In 1682, three-fourths of those who sat in this joint committee were Burgesses. This, of course, gave the lower house a preponderating influence in the committee and, consequently, a controlling voice in the determination of all

---

[12] The assembly restricted its judicial authority still farther by ordering in 1647 that the decisions of the Quarter Court were to be final for all causes coming up to it by appeal from the county courts. However, this restriction was afterwards set aside. Hening, Statutes at Large, I, 272, 334, 345, 398, 541; II, 65, 66, 266.

[13] This exception against Northampton County was afterwards repealed. Hening, Statutes at Large, I, 519, 520, 541, 575; II, 66, 362, 397. Virginia Magazine of History and Biography, VIII, 395.

causes referred to the assembly for trial. As the Burgesses
were chosen by the people, in practice, therefore, it resulted
that the highest court of appeal in the colony was an elect-
ive body, directly responsible to the people.[14]

The character of the justice meted out by the assembly
seems to have been in keeping with the spirit of the times.
Apparently it was neither milder nor severer than that
administered by the courts. The penalties inflicted for
criminal offenses were similar to those prescribed by the
Quarter and county courts. Fines were imposed and resort was had to the lash. Offenders were also punished by
suspension from office and disqualification for places of
profit or honor. The assembly, like the courts, sometimes
tried to coerce transgressors into repentance by requiring
them to ask forgiveness of the persons injured by them.[15]

Appeals to the assembly continued to be allowed until
about 1682, when they were stopped by order of the King.
At that time a dispute arose in the committee of justice between those of its members who were Burgesses and those
that were councillors, the Burgesses contending that the

---

[14] By the term "people," is not meant the whole adult male population, but only the voters. As a rule, the right to vote was allowed
to all freemen before 1670 and to freeholders only after that time.
But there were two exceptions to this rule: from 1655 to 1656 only
"housekeepers" were allowed to vote, and during Bacon's rebellion
this privilege was allowed to all freemen. Chandler, Hist. of
Suffrage in Va., J. H. U. Studies, XIX, 279-283. Hartwell, Blair,
and Chilton, Present State of Virgnia, 25, 26. Hening, II, 157.

[15] One case is reported (1662) which affords an instance of a dis-
regard on the part of the assembly of the rules of evidence which
would now be considered quite reprehensible. It seems that one
Anne Price had been tried in the county court of Elizabeth City,
and that a new hearing before the assembly had been granted. The
committee of justice in their report on the case declared that there
was not sufficient evidence to warrant a conviction according to law.
Nevertheless, the assembly ordered the court of Elizabeth City to
"rehear the cause and according as the presumptions of the offence
shall appear determine some means of punishment" not exceeding
two years of service. The reason given for this decision was that
the assembly considered that an example ought to be made of the
accused and feared that an acquittal might encourage some insolence. Hening, I, 157; II, 15, 33, 156-157, 162, 458-463. Sainsbury
MSS., 1660-1676, 196, 197. Ibid., 1677-1679, 106. Randolph MSS.,
252.

councillors, having already given their decisions in the General Court, should not again sit on the same cases in the committee of the assembly. It was very unfortunate that the legislature was divided at a time when the executive was anxious to enlarge its authority. Lord Culpeper, who was then governor of the colony, welcomed this opportunity to enhance his own power at the expense of the assembly. He, accordingly, reported the disagreement to England and procured an order abolishing appeals to the assembly.[16] The records that have been examined do not state whether this act discontinuing appeals to the assembly also deprived this body of its power to determine causes originally. But there is evidence of a negative character which goes to show that the assembly ceased to be a court of justice after this event. With the possible exception of one act of attainder, no mention has been found of the assembly's trying cases after this time. In an account of the judiciary given in Beverley's history of Virginia, published in 1705, all the courts of justice in the colony are alluded to; but nothing is said of the judicial powers of the assembly, which leads us to infer that it had no such powers at that time.[17] Indeed, it is not improbable that prior to 1682, the assembly had in practice limited its judicial activity to appellate causes; and in that case, the stoppage of appeals, of course, deprived it entirely of its privilege to act as a court of justice.

The assembly was loath to part with its judicial authority, and in 1691 wrote to the agent of the colony in England urging him to use his endeavors towards gaining the King's consent to a renewal of appeals.[18] This attempt to regain a lost privilege was apparently unsuccessful, and from this time on the judicial activity of the assembly seems to have been confined mainly to docking entails and granting per-

---

[16] Hartwell, Blair, and Chilton, Present State of Virginia, 25, 26. Sainsbury MSS., 1679-1682, 151.
[17] Beverley, History of Virginia. Book IV, pp. 20-26.
[18] Sainsbury MSS., 1640-1691, 387.

missions to alienate entailed estates, if indeed even these may
be termed judicial functions.[19]

The royal order that discontinued appeals to the assembly eliminated the only element of democracy that had lin-
gered in the judiciary since the Restoration. Henceforth
the people were to exercise no influence, except an indirect
and moral one, on the decisions of the courts. It is true
that prior to this time the people had had no voice (except
in the Commonwealth period) either directly or indirectly
in the choice of the judges of the county and General
courts; but if an act of injustice were committed in the
lower courts, it could be corrected by an appeal to the assembly. As the latter was the highest court of appeal in the
colony, and could set aside the decisions of the other tribunals, it was natural that the courts would try to conform to
the precedents set by the assembly in the determination of
the causes brought before them. For this reason, the influence exerted on the judiciary by the assembly, was in all
probability out of all proportion to the amount of judicial
business transacted by it. Of the two branches of the
legislature, the lower house, the representatives of the people, was much stronger numerically than the upper,[20] and, as
we have already seen, took the leading part in the trial of
appeals. Up until 1682, therefore, the Virginia judiciary
was aristocratic at the bottom and democratic at the top;
but the element of democracy introduced at the top must
have found its way, as an influence, into all the branches of
the judicial system. But now the only link that connected
the judiciary with direct responsibility to the people was
severed, and the judiciary was from this time on thoroughly
aristocratic in all its branches.

This curtailment of the power of the assembly made it
possible for the governor to exert an undue influence on the
judges of the General Court in their administration of jus-

---

[19] Hening, IV, 36, 50, 240, 307, 451-53, 534-37; V, 214-16, 277-84,
392-95.
[20] Hening, I, 288, 289.

tice. The General Court, which was composed of the governor and his council, was now the highest judicial authority in the colony.[21] The councillors were appointed by the King, and were in no sense responsible to the people. Besides it was to their interest to render such decisions as would be acceptable to the governor. There were a good many important offices at his disposal, and practically all of these were held by the members of the council. These places could easily be distributed in such a way as to reward his friends and punish his enemies. Therefore, dissent from the opinion of the governor might entail self-denial, while conformity with his views might mean reward.[22] But the power of the governor to influence judicial decisions could be curbed so long as appeals were allowed to the assembly. For if the governor by corrupt means should procure an unjust order from the General Court, it could be set aside by the assembly. But this check was removed when the judicial powers of the assembly were destroyed, and as a premium was put upon subservience to the wishes of the governor, it could hardly be expected that the Supreme Court would be entirely free from abuses.

According to an account of Virginia written about the end of the seventeenth century, the General Court fell into abuses immediately after appeals to the assembly were stopped. The authors of this account, Messrs. Hartwell, Blair, and Chilton, say that after appeals to the assembly were discontinued, the governor was usually able to get from the General Court such decisions as he desired, and that the people were, in consequence, sorely oppressed. But this book betrays strong prejudices and decided hostility to the governor, and, therefore, it is quite likely that what is said about the despotism of the governor is an exaggerated

---

[21] It is true that in important cases, appeals to the King were still allowed, but the inconvenience of prosecuting suits in England rendered this privilege of no great practical value.

[22] Hartwell, Blair, and Chilton, 22-24.

statement, to say the least.[23] But even if it is a correct representation of conditions as they were at that time, it does not follow that the General Court, from this time on, usually obeyed the dictates of the governor in its administration of justice. While it must be admitted that the stoppage of appeals to the assembly left unchecked a dangerous power in the hands of the governor, yet this power could not avail him much so long as a majority of the councillors were men of integrity and stamina. That the council was frequently, if not generally, composed principally of such men, we have every reason to believe. It cannot be said that their attitude towards the governor was, as a rule, one of tame acquiescence in the policies advocated by him; for we sometimes find them vigorously resisting the measures proposed by him.[24] It may, therefore, be safely inferred that the picture of the General Court that was drawn at the end of the seventeenth century was not a true likeness of this tribunal as it generally appeared in the eighteenth century.

Still, this does not alter the fact that there was always present in the judicial sysem a latent weakness which might develop into a dangerous abuse whenever the conditions were favorable. If a strong and unprincipled governor should at any time be joined with a weak or dishonest council, the General Court would be liable to develop symptoms of corruption. That the people suffered no greater injustice than they did is to be ascribed to the circumstance that this unfortunate union did not often take place, rather than to be attributed to any safeguards with which the Virginia constitution was provided.

APPEALS TO ENGLAND.

The assembly, even prior to 1682, was not the highest court to which the Virginians had access. The right to

---

[23] Hartwell, Blair, and Chilton, 26. We know, however, from other sources that abuses crept into the General Court about this time, but it does not appear that they were in any way connected with the influence wielded by the governor over the court. See p. 56.

[24] See pp. 40, 60-62.

appeal to England in important cases was one of the privileges enjoyed by them from the earliest period. Problems of justice sometimes arose in the colony for which the home judiciary offered no satisfactory solution, and so from time to time the mother country was called upon to assist in the administration of justice in Virginia. Before the Company was deprived of its governmental rights, it sometimes took part in the administration of justice in the colony. The appeals to the Company were usually in the form of complaints made by the colonists against acts of alleged injustice on the part of the governor, or of petitions from persons living in England, who claimed to have been wronged in their possessions in Virginia. The Company could set aside a decision given in Virginia if it were unjust and had not been rendered in accordance with their general instructions. It also sometimes ordered the governor and council to inquire into the alleged grievances of petitioners and to right the wrongs complained of.[25]

It is hardly safe to make any generalization regarding the methods employed by the Company in the performance of its judicial duties, owing to the fact that not many trials are recorded in its proceedings. It seems, however, from the few cases that are given, that the complaints of petitioners were referred to the Council of the Company for a preliminary hearing or for final determination. One instance is given in which the whole Company, assembled in a great Quarter Court, was called upon to decide an important case which had been brought up by appeal from Virginia. The Council brought in a report favoring a reversal of the decision given in Virginia, which was adopted by the Company almost unanimously.[26]

---

[25] Records of the Virginia Company, I, 48, 129; II, 11, 29, 39, 45, 46, 145.

[26] This case is of interest not only because it gives us an insight into the methods employed by the Company in the transaction of its judicial business, but also because it shows what was, at that time, the Company's opinion regarding the constitutionality of the military rule of Dale and Argoll.

The Company had no authority to try criminals that escaped from Virginia and returned to England.[27] But if any persons that had been sent from Virginia for criminal offenses or had come away by stealth, should circulate slanderous reports about the colony with the intent to bring it into disrepute, or should show any insolence to the Council, any two of the Council (the treasurer to be one) could have such evil-doers apprehended and brought before them for examination. If it should be proved that they were guilty of these misdemeanors, these Councillors could require them to give security for their good behavior, or could send them back to Virginia for trial.[28] The power to punish the colonial governors for malfeasance in office was not one of the privileges granted to the Company. Removal from office was the greatest penalty that it could inflict for the misrule of these governors. In 1621, John Smith favored inserting in a new patent for which the Company was going to ask a clause empowering the Company to punish the Virginia governors for their acts of injustice. This proposal was objected to on the ground that it would cause the new patent to be defeated in Parliament.[29]

In 1624, the charter of the Company was annulled, and Virginia was brought under the authority of the crown.

The history of the case begins in October, 1618, when a certain settler was sentenced to death in Virginia by a court martial. Governor Argoll was persuaded by some of the court not to execute the death sentence, and the accused was released on condition that he would leave the colony never to return, and would never speak disparagingly of Lord De La Warr, Argoll, or the plantation. An appeal was taken from this decision to the Council and Company in England. The Council (of the Company) sent to Yeardley (who was then governor of the colony) and the Virginia council this appeal and Argoll's answer, together with a letter from the Company, and ordered them to investigate the case and report their findings back to England. Finally (1620), the whole question was brought before the Company assembled in a Quarter Court. The Company, in giving its decision, declared that a trial by court martial was illegal. Records of Virginia Company, I, 48; II, 29, 30, 39-44, 45.

[27] Ibid., II, 159.
[28] Sainsbury MSS., 1573-1618, 160, 161.
[29] Proceedings of the Virginia Company, I, 113.

The King, the same year, appointed fifty-five commissioners and turned over to them the general management of the colony.[30] This board was probably too large for the proper supervision of colonial affairs, and in 1634, a smaller one, composed of thirteen members, was entrusted with the governmental control of the English colonies. This committee of thirteen was given power to remove governors, appoint judges, and establish courts, and was instructed to "hear and determine all manner of complaints from the colonies."[31] It was one of several intermediary boards which in turn looked after the affairs of the colonies. The most important of these intermediary bodies was the Board of Trade, which was organized in 1696.[32]

After 1624, appeals to England were made to the King and the Privy Council; but appeals as well as petitions and complaints, were, in the seventeenth century at least, frequently, if not generally, referred to the intermediary boards, which examined them and advised the action that should be taken on them by the King and the Privy Council. Appeals to the Privy Council were allowed in both civil and criminal cases, and complaints were sometimes made by citizens of England against acts of alleged injustice which had not been inquired into by the colonial courts.[33] How-

---

[30] Rymer, Foedera, XVII, 611-13.
[31] Sainsbury MSS., 1631-1637-8, 65.
[32] Brodhead, Documents Relating to the Colonial History of New York, Vol. III, Introduction, XIII-XIX.
[33] Va. Mag. of Hist. and Biography, XII, 12. William and Mary College Quarterly, IX, 98-100, 165. Hening, V, 292. Sainsbury MSS., 1624-1631, 230; ibid., 1631-1637, 54, 199; ibid., 1637-8-1649, 26, 27, 77, 82, 83; ibid., 1640-1691, 89, 292; ibid., 1660-1676, 138; ibid., 1677-1679, 86, 202; ibid., 1679-1682, 104, 155, 162, 188, 189, 213; ibid., 1682-1686. 221, 223; ibid., 1691-1697, 250.
It will be noticed that these references are mostly to the seventeenth century records. It was the custom for appeals to England to be tried by a committee of the Privy Council, known as the Lords of Appeals. Whether this committee in the eighteenth century really gave its own decisions or only confirmed the dicisions that had already been recommended by the intermediary board, I am unable to say; but it seems to have continued the old practice of requiring the opinion of the intermediary board on complaints coming before it from the colonies. Beverley, History of Va., Book IV, p. 21. Calendar Va. State Papers, I, 195.

ever, it seems that appeals to the Privy Council were not often allowed in criminal cases, as few of them are mentioned in the documents that have been examined. Beverley, the historian, whose work was published in 1705, said that he was not sure that appeals in criminal cases were ever allowed to the King and the Privy Council; but the records show that persons charged with penal offenses were sometimes sent to England for trial.[34] It was not intended that the intermediary boards should erect themselves into courts of justice for the trial of unimportant causes. They were to exercise only a general supervision over the administration of justice in the colonies. Besides, the best interests of the colonists demanded that disputes arising among themselves should be settled by the home judiciary, as suits could not be prosecuted in England except at considerable expense and inconvenience. But these natural restrictions were not the only limitations on appeals to the King. Before the end of the seventeenth century, appeals in civil cases had become limited to those suits in which the amounts involved exceeded three hundred pounds sterling.[35]

---

[34] Beverley, History of Va., Book IV, Chap. VI, p. 21. Sainsbury MSS., 1706-1714, 380. McDonald Papers, II, 166.
[35] Chalmers, Political Annals, 356. Dinwiddie Papers, I, 383, 384. In 1682, the limit was one hundred instead of three hundred pounds sterling. Sainsbury MSS., 1679-1682, 151.

CHAPTER II.

THE SUPERIOR COURTS.

THE QUARTER OR GENERAL COURT.

Next to the assembly in the order of jurisdiction came the Quarter Court, which was afterwards known as the General Court. This tribunal was the successor of the council court, which administered justice in the colony during the first few years of its existence. As the local council and its president were the judges of the Council Court, so the governor and his council constituted the Quarter or General Court. An exact date for the origin of the Quarter Court cannot be given. We know, however, that the governor and his council performed judicial duties as early as 1619,[1] and it is not improbable that Lord De La Warr and the military rulers who succeeded him advised with their councils in the administration of justice.

Not only is it difficult to say just when the councillors began to share with the governor the responsibilities of meting out justice, but it is also equally difficult to determine the precise date at which their executive and judicial duties began to be performed in separate sessions. In Governor Wyatt's instructions, given in 1621, there is an intimation that the governor and his council sat at different times as a court of justice and as a council of state. In these same instructions, the governor and council are ordered to " appoint proper times for the administration of justice "[2] From this, therefore, it would seem that as early as 1621 the governor and his council, as a rule, discharged their judicial duties while sitting as a court of justice and agreed on their executive measures while sitting as a council of

---

[1] Colonial Records of Virginia, 24, 28.
[2] Hening, I, 116, 117.

state. But if there was a line of cleavage separating the
judicial from the other business transacted by the council,
it could not, at first, have been a clearly defined one; for in
the early proceedings of the council we find judicial, executive, and legislative measures all recorded together.[3] Nor
can it be said that the executive and judicial sessions of the
council were held at different times of the year. The
councillors could not come together without considerable
inconvenience owing to the distance at which they lived
from each other,[4] and when they assembled, in all probability, they did not adjourn until they had despatched all
the business of every kind that was before them. Certain
days, or parts of days, were perhaps set apart for deciding
suits and others for performing executive duties.

During the first years of which we have any record of
them, the meetings of the council for the trial of causes
were held at irregular intervals.[5] It was not many years,
however, before a system of regular quarterly terms had
been evolved. When that stage was reached by the court,
the name Quarter Court could be properly used, and its
development in the direction of independence of the executive was practically complete, or rather about as nearly
complete as it was at any time during the colonial period.
But we are unable to say just when the court arrived at this
point in its development. A step towards quarter sessions
was taken in 1621, when the council was ordered by the
Company to assemble four times a year and remain in
session one week each time. These meetings were to be
devoted to "state affairs and law suits." This order came
in response to a complaint made by Governor Yeardley to
the effect that the councillors did not come together as often
as the public interests demanded. The reasons assigned by him
for this indifferent attendance were that they were few in

---

[3] Robinson MSS., 54, 59, 60, 63, 66, 67, 70, 73.
[4] See page 35.
[5] Virginia Court Book, 1622-1626.

number, lived at considerable distances from each other and received no compensation for their services in the colony.[6] By 1626 the term Quarter Court had come into use, being applied to the quarterly meetings of the councillors. But meetings of the council were also held in the intervals between the quarter terms, and at these, as well as at the quarter sessions, judicial duties were performed. Just how long before the judicial sessions of the council were confined to the quarter terms, cannot be determined, but it was probably not later than 1642.[7] By 1632 the Quarter Court had gone far enough in its development to receive statutory recognition. At that time a law was passed providing that the " foure quarter corts shall be held at James City yearlie, as followeth, vizt., uppon the first day of September, the first day of December, the first of March, and the first day of June." [8]

After this changes were made from time to time in the dates at which the courts convened.[9] In 1659, the June court was abolished because it was found inconvenient to hold it at that time. The reason given for this inconvenience was that " the shipps are (were) then out of the country, time of payment past, and the crop then chiefly in hand." The sessions of the Quarter Court were by this change reduced to three a year.[10] The term *Quarter Court* had now become a misnomer, and in a few years that of *General Court* was substituted for it.[11] It was afterwards considered unnecessary for the court to convene as often as three times a year, and in 1684, the sessions were made semi-annual. From that time on the court met regularly in April and October.[12]

The act of 1632 made no provision regarding the length

[6] Collingwood MSS., I, 236.
[7] Virginia Court Book, 1623-1626. Robinson MSS., 57, 62, 63, 65-67. Hening, I, 270. McDonald Papers, I, 377.
[8] Hening, I, 174.
[9] Ibid., I, 187, 270, 461, 524; II, 227; III, 289; V, 319, 320.
[10] Hening. I, 524.
[11] Ibid., II, 58.
[12] Hugh Jones, Present State of Virginia, 29. Dinwiddie Papers, I, 383. Hening, III, 10, 289; V, 319, 320; VI, 328.

of the terms of the court. In the instructions given by the King in 1639 to Governor Wyatt, the Quarter Courts were required to remain in session one week or longer if necessary.[12] About four years later, it was enacted by the assembly that the four courts (which at that time were appointed to be held in March, June, October, and November) should continue, the first and last for eighteen days each, and the second and third, for ten days each. There was also a provision requiring the assignment of a definite number of causes instituted by writs for each day of every term.[14] In imposing these minute regulations on the court, the assembly acted as if the amount of judicial business to be dispatched by the governor and council each year was a constant quantity which could be measured in advance with mathematical accuracy. After this the length of the terms was changed from time to time, but was finally fixed at twenty-four days exclusive of Sundays, though the court was not required to remain in session so long if it could clear its docket in a shorter time than that prescribed.[15]

It is not to be supposed that these inelastic regulations of the assembly could be closely fitted to the conditions with which the General Court had to deal. The assembly, of course, could not gauge beforehand the exact volume of the judicial business that would come before the court, and the attempts to limit it as to the number of causes it should try each day, or the number of days it should sit, must have been futile. We are not surprised, therefore, to find that during the periods for which we have a record of its proceedings, the General Court did not conform strictly to the statutory regulations regarding the times for meeting.[16]

---

[12] Sainsbury MSS. 1637-1649, 44.

[14] Hening, I, 270, 271.

[15] Hening, III, 289; V, 319, 320; VI, 328. Webb's Justice, 106.

[16] During the years 1674 and 1675, the meetings of the General Court were held on the following dates: 1674—April 2, 3, 4, 6, 7, 8, 9; Sept. 22, 23, 24, 25, 26, 28, 29; Oct. 1, 2, 5, 8; Nov. 16, 17, 19, 20, 21. 1675—March 1, 3, 4, 5, 6; June 15, 16, 17, 18, 19; Oct. 4, 5, 6, 7, 8, 9, 11, 12.

At this time the statutes provided that three courts should be held

The General Court usually held its sessions at the capital of the colony, that is, at Jamestown during the seventeenth century, and at Williamsburg during the remainder of the colonial period.[17] In the early years there seems to have been no state-house in Virginia, and the business of government was transacted at the house of the governor. The governor was also put to great expense in entertaining councillors and Burgesses during the terms of the Quarter Court and the assembly, and he was authorized by the King to recoup himself by appropriating to his own use all the fines imposed by the court. But the incomes from the fines apparently fell far short of the outgo occasioned by the hospitality which was dispensed at public times. For we find Governor Harvey writing to England in a despairing tone saying that if some relief were not soon afforded him the expense of council meetings and assemblies would, as he phrased it, cause both his heart and his credit to break, and that he should be called the host, rather than the Governor of Virginia.[18] In 1639, Governor Wyatt was instructed by the King to have a state-house built,[19] but this order was either not carried out, or, if it was, the building erected was destroyed by fire. For in 1663, the sessions of the General Court and the assembly were being held in ale-houses. High rents had to be paid for the use of these places; and, besides, it was considered beneath the dignity of the colony

---

every year. According to laws enacted in 1662 and 1666, the terms of these courts were to begin April 15, September 20, and November 20, unless those dates fell on Saturday or Sunday, in which case they were to begin the following Monday. The length of the first term was to be eighteen days, that of the other two, twelve days each. This contrast between the regularity found in the legal provisions and the irregularity found in the court practices, goes to show that the assembly did not succeed in its efforts to place the General Court in a strait-jacket. Records of the General Court, 1670-1676; see dates given above. Robinson MSS., 68-74. Records of York Co., 1633-1694, 20, 54, 101. Hening, II, 58, 59, 227.
[17] Records General Court, 1670-1676, 154. Robinson MSS., 51, 59, 69, 74. Hugh Jones, Present State of Virginia, 25. Hening, III, 200.
[18] MacDonald Papers, II, 23. Sainsbury MSS., 1631-1636, 35.
[19] Sainsbury MSS., 1637-8-1649, 46.

38   *Justice in Colonial Virginia.*

for its laws to be made and its justice administered in
houses where drinks were vended. For these reasons, the
assembly in this same year passed a law providing for the
erection of a building in which the affairs of the colony
could be conducted.[20] After Williamsburg became the colonial capital, a costly state-house was built, the finest, it is
said, that could then be seen in the British posessions in
North America. One side of the capitol was given over to
the use of the General Court and its officers, and the other to
the assembly and its officers.[21]

As we have already seen, the General Court was composed
of the governor and his council. Councillors were appointed by the Company before its charter was annulled and after
that time by the King on the recommendation of the intermediary boards. Vacancies in the council were usually filled
in the following manner:—the governor would select such
men as he deemed suitable for the office and would send in
their names, together with an account of their qualifications,
to the intermediary board;[22] when the list recommended
had received the sanction of this board, it was passed on to
the King, whose formal approval was necessary to make the
appointments legal. Councillors were not chosen for any
definite period, but were recommissioned whenever a new
governor was sent to the colony or a new King came to the
throne. The old councillors, however, were usually continued in office by the new commissions, and, in practice,
therefore, it resulted that the judges of the General Court
held office for life.[23]

[20] Hening, I, 425; II, 204.
[21] Sainsbury MSS., 1625-1705, 74. Hening, III, 419, 421. Hugh
Jones, Present State of Virginia, 25, 29. It took some time to complete the new capitol, and during the period of waiting the assembly,
and probably the General Court, held their sessions in the College
of William and Mary. Hening, III, 189, 197, 200, 204, 218, 224, 227,
419. Calendar of Virginia State Papers, I, 72, 73.
[22] These nominations were sometimes, if not generally, made with
the advice and consent of the Council. Sainsbury MSS., 1637-1649,
40. Spottswood's Letters, I, 7.
[23] Sainsbury MSS., 1606-1740, 104; ibid., 1624-1631, 138; ibid.,
1625-1705, 94, 118; ibid., 1625-1715, 373; ibid., 1631-1637, 183; ibid.,

By this method of appointment, the nominations made by the governor could not receive final confirmation until after a considerable period of time had elapsed. But it was important that the vacancies should not remain open during the period of waiting, and so the practice arose of allowing the governors to bridge over these intervals by making temporary appointments. Whenever the membership of the council was reduced by deaths or removals so as to be less than nine, the governor was to name as councillors as many prominent men as would be necessary to bring it back to that number. These temporary appointments became permanent after they had been confirmed by the King. The governor could also suspend councillors for just cause, but whenever he exercised this power, he had to report to England the reasons for his actions and support with proofs his charges against the excluded member.[24]

One would think that this power to suspend judges was liable to be abused by an unscrupulous governor. It would seem that by temporarily removing from the council those

---

1637-1649, 38, 40-42; ibid., 1679-1682, 125, 127, 135; ibid., 1691-1697, 176, 234; ibid., 1705-1707, 314, 524; ibid., 1706-1714, 334, 341. Va. Mag. of Hist. and Biog., II, 396. Proceedings of Va. Company, I, 76. Stith, Hist. of Va., Appendix, 32, 33. Randolph MS., 193, 200, 201, 406, 461-62, 482. De Jarnette Papers, II, 436, 535. Council Journal, 1721-1734, 32, 76, 91, 249, 252.

[24] Sainsbury MSS., 1640-1691, 318, 333, 396; ibid., 1682-3-1686, 28; ibid., 1686-1688, 30, 31; ibid., 1691-1697, 152; ibid., 1706-1714, 48; ibid., 1715-1720, 732, 788. Randolph MSS., 406. Calendar of Virginia State Papers, I, 1652-1681, 21. Spottswood's Letters, II, 54, 55. McDonald Papers, VI, 227.

According to accounts of Virginia written by Beverley and by Hartwell, Blair, and Chilton (published in 1705 and 1727, respectively), the power to suspend councillors was not conferred on the governors until after Bacon's Rebellion. As a reason for thus increasing the authority of the governor, it was contended that this power would enable him the better to put down an incipient rebellion. The rebellion of 1676, it was claimed, could have been nipped in the bud if Governor Berkeley had had the authority to suspend Bacon from the council. But instances are recorded in which councillors were suspended before Bacon's rebellion. Even Governor Berkeley himself exercised this power, for we find that in May, 1676, he issued a proclamation suspending Bacon from the council. Sainsbury MSS., 1624-1631, 111, 112, 216; ibid., 1660-1676, 244; ibid., 1677-1679, 19. Hartwell, Blair, and Chilton, 23, 56. Beverley, Hist. of Va., Book IV, Chap. I, p. 2.

members that opposed his schemes he might frequently procure unjust sentences from the court. But the council was
in a position to restrain him from an arbitrary use of this
power. The councillors were generally men of means and
influence, for none but those who were possessed of considerable estates were eligible to this high office.[25] One of
their number, usually the oldest in commission, succeeded
temporarily to the governor's chair when it became vacant
by the death or removal of the governor.[26] Many of them,
therefore, must have had considerable influence with the
governing authorities in England. An unjust removal was
always liable to bring on a quarrel between the injured
party and the governor, and in disputes of this kind the
governor was not always sustained by the King.[27] Besides,
the council, owing to the prominence of its members and
their family connections with other prominent men, had
great influence in the colony and was able to make its power
felt in the government.[28] Nor were the councillors slow in
asserting their rights. Their cavalier sentiments did not
prevent their antagonizing the King's representative when
they considered that their privileges had been infringed.
Consequently, they often took an attitude of strenuous opposition to the measures proposed by the governor. Indeed,
in the contests between the Virginia council and the King's
representative, the history of the struggles of the ancient
English kings with their barons was, in a small way, repeat-
ing itself. Sometimes these barons of Virginia and their
allies carried their opposition to the governor to the point of
procuring his dismissal.[29] We can, therefore, readily see

[25] Sainsbury MSS., 1640-1691, 438; ibid., 1691-1697, 152; ibid.,
1625-1715, 77. Spottswood's Letters, II, 39, 41, 55. McDonald
Papers, VI, 26.
[26] Sainsbury MSS., 1624-1631, 166, 216; ibid., 1637-1649, 38; ibid.,
1691-1697, 161; ibid., 1720-1730, 212. Randolph MSS., 413, 513.
[27] Sainsbury MSS., 1691-1697, 236. Hartwell, Blair, and Chilton,
36. Calendar of Virginia State Papers, I, 195.
[28] Sainsbury MSS., 1715-1720, 709.
[29] In the quarrel between Governor Harvey and his council, the
opposition verged upon rebellion. This dispute seems to have arisen

that the governor, even though he were unscrupulous, would, as far as he could, avoid every occasion to arouse the opposition of his council and would be very chary in the exercise of his power to suspend judges of the General Court.

During the Commonwealth period the method of choosing councillors was different from that employed at other times. While the colony was under the rule of Cromwell, the members of the council were appointed by the Burgesses, the representatives of the people. As the governor was also elected by the lower house, the Quarter Court enjoyed complete independence of the mother country during this time.[30] The effect of this change was to give to the people, indirectly through the House of Burgesses, power over the Quarter Court. It was a step towards democracy. The reforms in Virginia which gave the people a stronger voice in their government was a faint echo of the Puritan Revolution. But this impress of democracy which was dimly

out of a false conception on the part of the governor as to the relative powers of the chief executive officer and his cabinet, though Matthews, one of the opposing party, represents him as a tyrant who tried to lord it over the council. It is not unlikely that Harvey's support of the claims of the Maryland colony to Kent Island against those of Clayborne was also one of the causes of the rupture between him and his council. According to Matthews, Harvey claimed that the council had only the power to advise the governor, who could accept or reject its counsel as he saw fit. Harvey, on the other hand, declared that the council wanted to deprive him of his right to vote in the council except in case of a tie. There was no attorney-general in Virginia to decide the disputed question, and Harvey wrote to England for a legal opinion regarding the respective powers of the governor and council. The councillors believed their quarrel just, and, being supported by the Burgesses, deposed the governor and sent him to England to answer certain charges which they had brought against him. The King, of course, did not countenance such an attack, though indirect, on his royal prerogative, and sent Harvey back to Virginia as governor, and summoned some of the councillors who lead the opposition to England to " answer an information at the King's suit " in the Court of Star Chamber. No record has been found of any sentence being pronounced against them by this court, but two of them were detained in England a long time and were thus put to great inconvenience. Sainsbury MSS., 1631-1637, 1, 2, 111-116, 122-124, 126-130, 207, 210; ibid., 1640-1691, 2.

[30] Hening, I, 371, 372, 408, 422, 431, 504, 515, 517, 531.

stamped on the Virginia judiciary was soon effaced by the
royalist reaction. With the Restoration there came a return
to the old régime, and from that time until our own Revolution the people took no part either directly or indirectly in
the appointment of the judges of their most important
court.

A full council was usually composed of twelve or thirteen
members, though the number was sometimes greater and
sometimes less than this. During the early years, there
seems to have been no minimum limit below which the number could not be reduced by deaths and removals.[21] But
later there was a provision that the governor was to keep the
number up to nine by making temporary appointmets. The
attendance of the judges at the meetings of the General
Court was usually poor, considering their number, and
during the periods for which we have records of its proceedings, the court was generally attended only by about
one-half of the councillors.[22] But a certain number of judges

[21] Under the rule of Governor Pott, the number of councillors at
one time (1630) fell to two, but this was an exceptional case. Sainsbury MSS., 1624-1631, 129, 223; ibid., 1677-1679, 102; ibid., 1705-
1707, 314, 524. De Jarnette Papers, II, 436, 535. Winder MSS., I,
205. Randolph MSS., 193, 200, 201. Blair, Hartwell, and Chilton, 34,
35. Hening, II, 511. Beverley, Hist. of Va., Book IV, Chap. I,
p. 5.

[22] The only records now extant of the proceedings of the General
Court, except occasional notices, are the following: (1) A manuscript now in the Congressional Libary, known as the "Virginia
Court Book." It covers the period from March, 1623, to 1630 (?),
but only the first part of it is at present in a condition to be used.
(2) The General Court Records (1670-1676) in the library of the
Virginia Historical Society, Richmond. (3) The Robinson MSS.
(1626-1670), also in the library of the Virginia Historical Society.
These consist of notes made by Mr. Conway Robinson from the
original records of the council, probably from the MSS. now in the
Congressional Library. In addition to these there is given in one
volume of the Ludwell MSS. (in the library of the Virginia Historical
Society), a list of the cases tried in the General Court during a
brief period (1724-1726).
From these records, I find that the average attendance of councillors at courts, not including the governor, who was usually present,
was about six for the year beginning with May, 1624, and ending
with May, 1625, and a little below six for the period extending from
October, 1673, to March, 1676. Robinson MSS., 51-74. General
Court Records, 1670-1676, 154-261. Virginia Court Book, 1623-
1626, 20-95.

had to be present at every court before any case could be tried. No council could transact any business unless at least three of its members were present, and except on extra-ordinary occasions, no court could be held with a smaller quorum than five.[33] The failure on the part of the judges to attend the court sessions regularly was doubtless due mainly to the distance at which they lived from the seat of government and to the lack of travelling facilities.[34] In the early years the Quarter Court tried to coerce its judges into a better attendance by imposing fines on absentees, but apparently with little success.[35]

The councillors at first received no allowance for looking after the affairs of the colony, and, as we have seen, this was, according to Governor Yeardley, partly the cause of the poor attendance at the council meetings complained of by him.[36] The Company must have acted favorably on Yeardley's hint, for in 1625 we find the councillors receiving pay for their services.[37] A little later (1640) each one was granted exemption for himself and ten servants from all general taxes except ministers' dues and contributions for building churches or towns and for carrying on defensive wars.[38] To this privilege was afterwards added a salary of 250 pounds sterling, which was to be apportioned among the councillors according to their attendance at Quarter Courts and assemblies. By Bacon's laws the exemption from taxation was done away with, and one hundred pounds was added to the allowance that had hitherto been made to them. Other increases in salary were afterwards made, and

---

[33] Sainsbury MSS., 1625-1715, 77. Winder MSS., I, 205. Randolph MSS., 406, 435, 489. Dinwiddie Papers, I, 383.

[34] Collingwood MSS., I, 236.

[35] On one occasion the court was anxious that all the judges should be present at the next session, as an important case would then come up for trial, and in order to insure a full attendance, it ordered that every one that should be absent without a lawful excuse, should pay a fine of £40. Robinson MSS., 76, 186.

[36] Proceedings of Virginia Company, I, 126.

[37] Virginia Court Book, 1623-1626, 77.

[38] McDonald Papers, I, 379. Hening, I, 228, 445, 279.

in 1755, the services of the councillors were rewarded with more than twelve hundred pounds a year.[39]

In addition to the salary, there were other emoluments that went with the place of councillor. The councillors had almost an entire monoply of the principal places of honor and profit in the colony. They usually commanded the militia of their respective counties with the rank of colonel.[40] According to Hartwell, Blair, and Chilton, another source of profit to the members of the council was the privilege— shared also by the governor and the auditor—of buying at a low price all the quit-rents due to the King, which were paid in tobacco. The whole colony was divided among them, each commissioner taking the county or counties most convenient to him.[41]

The governor presided over the General Court and passed sentence on convicted criminals.[42] Causes were decided by a majority vote of the judges present, and when the councillors were equally divided, the deciding vote was cast by the governor.[43] There were also certain judicial duties that the governor could perform out of court. He could remit fines and forfeitures and grant pardons for all offenses except wilful murder and treason. Persons convicted of these crimes could be pardoned only by the King, but could be reprieved by the governor.[44] But these, as well as other

[39] Robinson MSS., 227, 228. Hening, I, 523; II, 32, 84, 85, 359, 391, 392; III, 348; V, 227. Sainsbury MSS., 1637-1649, 45; ibid., 1691-1697, 331. Dinwiddie Papers, I, 390. Beverley, Hist. and Present State of Va., Book IV, p. 6.

[40] Winder MSS., I, 206. Hartwell, Blair, and Chilton, 32, 33, 63.

[41] The quit-rents were an annual tax of one shilling on every fifty acres of land that had been patented. Hartwell, Blair, and Chilton, 33, 56, 57. Sainsbury MSS., 1691-1697, 342.

[42] Hartwell, Blair, and Chilton, 20, 21. General Court Records, 1670-1676, 53.

[43] Sainsbury MSS., 1624-1631, 134. Randolph MSS., 163, 207. McDonald Papers, I, 377. Spottswood's Letters, II, 14.

[44] It is true that Governor Pott pardoned wilful murder, but in doing so he exceeded his authority. In 1690 Governor Lord Howard was ordered not to remit fines above the amount of £10 without special permission from the King. Sainsbury MSS., 1624-1631, 216, 224, 225; ibid., 1640-1691, 320; ibid., 1682-1686, 3; ibid., 1720-1730,

judicial acts, seem usually to have been done with the advice of the council. Another power exercised by the governor was that of signing orders for the administration of estates and the execution of wills.⁴⁵ By an abuse of this privilege, Governor Howard was able to extort a tax from the people for his own private use. A high fee was charged every time the seal was affixed to letters of administration and probates of wills. He claimed that the fees complained of were charged in all the colonies and that the revenue accruing from them was one of the perquisites of his office. The tax was such a burden that the Virginians sent Philip Ludwell to England to make complaints against the governor, but he did not succeed in procuring his dismissal.⁴⁶

The Quarter or General Court took cognizance of both civil and criminal causes, and its jurisdiction was both original and appellate. At first the governor and council decided causes of all kinds, but they were relieved of much of the judicial business of the colony after the county courts had grown into importance. It was some years, however, after the formation of the lower courts before we find any provisions restricting either the original or appellate jurisdiction of the Quarter Court with respect to suits of minor impor-

---

347, 392, 418, 465. Dinwiddie Papers, I, 384, 385. Randolph MSS., 138, 408, 416, 464. Council Journal, 1721-1734, 220, 221, 251, 267, 280, 283, 341, 412, 413, 494, 495.

⁴⁵ Certificates for granting letters of administration were given both by the General Court and by the county courts. When an administrator or executor had obtained such a certificate from a court, it was presented to the governor, who thereupon signed an order empowering him to administer the estate mentioned in the certificate. For a while the justices of the county courts had the power to sign letters of administration. A law was passed in 1676, which was re-enacted next year, authorizing any two justices of the quorum to sign probates and letters of administration. General Court Records, 1670-1676, 185, 213. Henrico County Court Records, 1737-1746, 15, 34, 135, 249, 359, 412; ibid., 1719-1724, 28, 88, 294, 335. Rappahannock County Court Records, 1686-1692, 15, 24, 74, 156, 230. Essex County Court Records, 1695-1699, 49, 95, 100, 122. Henrico County Court Records, 1677-1692, 16, 17. Blair, Hartwell, and Chilton, 47, 48. Hening, II, 359, 391. Beverley, Hist. of Va., Book IV, p. 29.

⁴⁶ Beverley, Book I, pp. 89-90. McDonald Papers, VII, 154, 155.

tance. But the judicial work to be performed could not be properly apportioned between the higher and lower tribunals without narrowing the jurisdiction of the former. So, before the middle of the century was reached, the original jurisdiction of the Quarter Court began to be restricted so as to exclude all unimportant civil causes. The laws imposing this limitation varied from time to time, but always provided that only suits involving certain amounts could originate in the higher court. The civil causes which these regulations allowed to be brought directly into the General Court were those in which the amounts involved equalled or exceeded ten, fifteen, sixteen, or twenty pounds sterling— these were the different limits at different times.[47]

When the monthly courts were first organized there were no restrictions on appeals from them to the Quarter Court, and any one who was not satisfied with the award of the monthly court could bring his case by appeal before the governor and council for a hearing.[48] It was not many years, however, before the appellate, like the original, jurisdiction of the Quarter Court began to be narrowed down to the more important cases. By a law of 1647, the appellate jurisdiction of the governor and council was limited to controversies involving amounts not less than sixteen hundred pounds of tobacco, or ten pounds sterling, but appeals from Northampton, a county east of Chesapeake Bay, were not to be allowed on account of its remoteness from James City, except in causes of double that amount.[49] But this restriction was found impracticable, and some years later it was repealed,

---

[47] Hening, I, 125, 346, 477; III, 143, 144, 289; V, 469; VI, 327. Dinwiddie Papers, I, 383. Beverley, Book VI, p. 24.

[48] Hening, I, 125.

[49] So far as I have been able to find, there was no law thus restricting appeals before 1647; but a limitation had existed in the practice of the courts for a few years prior to this time. In 1642, Governor Berkeley, in his commission to the justices of Lower Norfolk County, instructed them to allow no appeals to the governor and council for amounts not exceeding 600 pounds of tobacco or ten pounds sterling. Lower Norfolk County Records, 1637-1643, 160. Hening I, 345, 398, 520.

except that part of it that applied to Northampton county.[50] One of the reforms instituted by the legislaure of 1676 was the removal of this discrimination against the trans-Chesapeake counties.[51] In the eighteenth century appeals to the Quarter Court were again limited so as to exclude unimportant cases, and this restriction continued in force until the end of the colonial period.[52]

The appellate jurisdiction of the General Court was also limited in another way. The appellant always had to pay heavy damages when the governor and council affirmed the decision of the lower court. At first the law provided that all persons appealing from the monthly courts to the governor and council should pay double damages when cast in their suits.[53] But a proper administration of justice demanded that the principal tribunal should not be walled in too closely against suits originating in the lower courts, and so it was afterwards found necessary to lower the barriers by which they were kept out. By a statute of 1647, the burdens borne by appeals to the Quarter Court were reduced to fifty per cent additional damages.[54] But even this law left the General Court too much hampered in the exercise of its appellate jurisdiction, and before the end of the century, the damages on appeals had become fixed at fifteen per cent of the amount originally awarded by the lower court.[55]

---

[50] Hening, I, 541; II, 66. Hartwell, Blair, and Chilton, 46. General Court Records, 1670-1676, 33, 71.

[51] Hening, II, 362, 397. The legislature that met in June, 1676, was under the influence of Bacon, and the laws passed by it are known as Bacon's Laws. All these were repealed the next year, but many of them were re-enacted. Hening, II, 341.

[52] Hening, III, 300; IV, 188; V, 481; VI, 339. Mercer, Va. Laws, 8, 9. [53] Hening, I, 125. [54] Ibid., I, 345.

[55] From this time on the damages to be paid by the defendant when an appeal was decided against him was fifteen per cent of the amount first awarded in all personal and mixed actions. In the early part of the eighteenth century, the damages in real actions were fixed at 2000 pounds of tobacco for every case appealed. During the last years of the colonial period, a difference as to the amount of damages charged was made between the appeals of the plaintiff and those of the defendant. The former had to pay fifty shillings, or 500 pounds of tobacco, whenever the appellate decision was against him. Hening, III, 143, 301, 514; V, 480; VI, 340. Mercer, Virginia Laws, 10.

There were never any separate chancery courts in Virginia during the colonial period, but both the General Court and the lower tribunals sat on chancery cases. If any one were wronged by a decision at common law, he could be granted a new hearing in chancery; but his cause would be tried by the same judges sitting as a court of chancery.[56] This was the usual practice, but when Lord Howard was governor an attempt was made to introduce a more imposing method of deciding chancery suits. It was his aim to establish an independent court for the trial of chancery cases, over which the governor was to preside as Lord Chancellor. The councillors sat with him, but were expected to give advice only, as the governor reserved to himself the sole power of rendering decisions. In order that this chancery court might appear the more independent of the General Court, the governor convened it, not in the state-house where the sessions of the latter were held, but in the dining-room of a private house. But this high court of chancery was short-lived. After Lord Howard ceased to be governor, the General Court resumed its old practice of deciding chancery causes.[57]

During the greater part of the seventeenth century, the General Court and the assembly were the only courts in the colony that could punish important criminal offenses, those affecting life or member.[58] The criminal jurisdiction of the Quarter Court also extended to minor offenses, though these were also cognizable in the county courts. Indeed, neither law nor custom recognized any sharp dividing line between the jurisdiction of the higher and lower tribunals in criminal cases. In the early records of the Quarter Court, we

[56] Blair, Hartwell, and Chilton, 43. Ludwell Papers, Vol. III. Records of Henrico County, 1719-1724, 47, 109, 129, 148, 370; ibid., 1710-1714, 74, 252, 306. Mercer, Virginia Laws, 9, 156.

[57] Beverley, History of Va., Book I, pp. 90-91. Hartwell, Blair, and Chilton, 20. Sainsbury MSS., 1691-1697, 335.

[58] The county courts were for a while permitted to try important criminal cases, but they were deprived of this power in 1656. Hening, I, 397, 398.

meet with many of the same class of law-breakers that appear in the order-books of the county courts.[59]

In the Quarter Court, even at an early period, persons charged with grave offenses were tried by a petit jury after they had been indicted by a grand jury.[60] It could not be expected, however, that information of all the crimes committed in the colony would reach the grand jury without the aid of some intermediary agency. Besides, it was impossible for the sheriff that attended the General Court to make arrests in distant counties. Therefore, the judicial machinery of the counties had to be employed in bringing criminals before the governor and council for trial. Arrests for crimes were made by the sheriffs of the counties in which they were committed, and criminal offenses were first inquired into by the justices of the peace, who decided which cases should be tried by the county courts, and which ones should have a hearing before the governor and council.[61]

In the early years, certain offenses, chiefly breaches of the moral code, could also be brought before the governor and council by the churchwardens. These officers were to report all those who had been guilty during the year, of drunkenness, adultery, swearing, absence from church, Sabbath-breaking, and other sins of like character, as well as ministers who had failed to preach one sermon every Sunday, and " such maysters and mistresses as had been (shall be) delinquent in the catechising the youth and ignorant persons." But the practice of receiving presentments made by churchwardens seems to have been discontinued by the court before the middle of the seventeenth century.[62]

---

[59] General Court Records, 1670-1676, 155, 156, 187, 211, 222. Records of Lower Norfolk County, 1637-1643, 2, 5, 15, 52, 62, 103, 177, 218. Records of Accomac County, 1640-1645, 49, 69, 88, 97, 168, 200. Robinson MS., 8, 11, 30, 76, 78. Records of Rappahannock County, 1686-1692, 55, 111, 114, 147, 158.

[60] Robinson MSS., 75, 76, 83. For an account of jury trials in the General Court and the oyer and terminer courts, see pp. 66-68.

[61] Records of Accomac County, 1632-1640, 43, 47; ibid., 1640-1645, 270. Hening, I, 304; III, 225, 389-391. Records of Rappahannock County, 1686-1692, 162, 163. See p. 96.

[62] Hening, I, 125, 155, 156, 180. Robinson MSS., 220.

The Virginia courts were governed in their decisions by
the common law of England and by the Parliamentary statutes that were enacted before the colony was settled, but not
by any that were enacted after that event except those that
made mention of the plantations.[63] The first act of assembly
that has been found in which the common law of England
is recognized as being in force in Virginia was passed in
1662;[64] but in all probability the common law was to some
extent observed by the courts during the entire colonial
period with the exception of the time during which the
colony was under military rule. One would naturally expect the early judges to decide cases according to the laws
under which they had lived in England, in so far as they
knew them, even if they were not required to do so. Besides, prior to 1662 orders were issued from England from
time to time directing the authorities in Virginia to follow
the laws of England, as far as was practicable, in their government of the colony. Such an instruction was given to
the King's council of Virginia in 1606, and a similar provision is found in commissions to governors that were issued
before 1662. As early as 1621, Governor Wyatt was instructed to " do justice after the form of the laws of England." [65] The benefit of the writ of *habeas corpus* was not
formally extended to Virginia until 1710, when this privilege
was brought over to the colonists by Lieutenant-Governor
Spottswood.[66] But this privilege was enjoyed in Virginia before this formal recognition of it was made by the crown;

[63] Byrd MSS., ed. 1866, II, 237. Records Lower Norfolk County,
1637-1643, 160. Accomac County Records, 1640-1645, 149.
In 1711, a woman was brought before the General Court for violating a penal law passed by Parliament in the twenty-first year of
the reign of James I. The case was dismissed on the ground that
the law did not apply to Virginia, as it was passed after the colony
was settled and the plantations were not mentioned in it. Spottswood's Letters, II, 57, 58.
[64] Hening, II, 43.
[65] Brown, Genesis of the United States, 66. McDonald Papers, I,
376. Sainsbury MSS., 1637-1649, 44. Hening, I, 44.
[66] Spottswood's Letters, II, 13. Henrico County Court Records,
1710-1714, 28. Journal of the Assembly, 1697-1720, 36-37.

for a writ of *habeas corpus* was granted to Major Robert Beverley in 1682.[67]

While the General Court doubtless tried to conform its decisions to the laws of England, yet it was impossible to fit the judicial business of the colony into exactly the same mold into which that of the mother country had been cast. A certain amount of elasticity had to be given to the laws of England before they could be adapted to the differing conditions in Virginia.[68] Besides, a legal education was not a requisite qualification for membership in the council, and so cases must sometimes have arisen in which the judges did not know how to apply the common law. Then, too, during the greater part of the seventeenth century, the legal profession maintained with difficulty its existence in the face of the opposition which it encountered from the assembly, and, therefore, the judges for most of this time were without legal advice from professional attorneys as to the proper interpretation of laws and precedents.[69] The Virginia statutes did not, of course, cover all the offenses of which the court took cognizance, consequently, and especially in the early years, it had to rely mainly on its own originality in rendering decisions.

The Quarter Court did not believe in half measures when it came to dealing out punishment to those who had incurred its censure, and the severity of some of its early sentences leaves the impression that the spirit of Dale was at that time still lingering in the Virginia judiciary. Some of the inhuman penalties inflicted by the High Marshal are recorded in the early proceedings of the Quarter Court. Offenders

---

[67] Hening, III, 547. Campbell says that his privilege had been denied the Virginians prior to this time. He probably overlooked the case cited above. Campbell, History of Virginia, 379.

[68] Hening, II, 43.

[69] See pp. 116-118. However, the court was not entirely without legal advice, for there was an attorney-general in the colony as early as 1643. Virginia Magazine of History and Biography, VIII, 70.

were made to lie neck and heels together,[70] or were made to
stand in the pillory, sometimes with their ears nailed to it.[71]
The death penalty usually took the form of hanging, but one
case is mentioned in which the criminal was ordered to be
drawn and hanged.[72] One way in which fornication had to
be atoned for was for the sinner to do penance in church
during divine worship by standing before the congregation
wrapped in a white sheet.[73] Particularly severe was the punishment inflicted on those who spoke disrespectfully of the
government authorities. That the early councillors were
not inclined to tolerate seditious utterances on the part of
the people and were not troubled with nice scruples regarding the freedom of speech, can be seen from the manner in
which they disposed of the following case, which came before them in 1624. A man who had used abusive language
in speaking about Governor Wyatt was arraigned before the
council in the absence of the governor, who refrained from
taking part in the proceedings. In punishing this insult to
its president the court ordered that the tongue of the
offender should be bored through with an awl, and that he
should also " pass through a guard of forty men, should

[70] One case is recorded in which the culprit had to lie in this
position for twelve hours. Robinson MS., 65, 76.
[71] This ignominious punishment was not confined to servants and
criminals of the baser sort, but those that were high in authority
might be subjected to it. In 1624, we find the governor and council prescribing this penalty for their secretary, who had violated the
oath of secrecy that had to be taken by all who attended the council meetings by giving the King copies of their proceedings. As a
punishment for this betrayal of their secrets, the governor and council ordered that the secretary should stand in the pillory at James
City with both his ears nailed to it and then have them cut off.
The rigor of this sentence, however, was somewhat abated in the
execution, and the offending clerk escaped by losing only a piece of
one of his ears. Sainsbury MSS., 1624-1631, 112. Virginia Court
Book, 1623-1626, May, 1624. Robinson MSS., 28, 61.
[72] Robinson MSS., 75, 76.
[73] The Quarter Court, as well as the county courts, sometimes employed original methods of punishment. On one occasion a woman
was sentenced to be dragged at the stern of a boat to the *Margaret
and John,* a vessel anchored in James River. Another woman was
to be towed around the same vesel and then ducked three times.
Robinson MSS., 30, 53, 62, 65.

(shall) be butted by every one of them, at the head of the troop kicked and footed out of the fort; that he shall be banished out of James City and the Plantation, that he shall not be capable of any priviledge or freedome of the country," &c."

There were certain inherent weaknesses in the constitution of the General Court which were liable to breed abuse. Its close connection with the legislature and the executive was not favorable to an impartial administration of justice. The councillors, as members of the upper house of the assembly, took part in the enactment of the laws; as judges of the General Court they interpreted them; and as advisers of the governor assisted in the execution of them. Such a union of separate and distinct powers in one body of men deprived the judiciary of that independence which, according to modern views, is so essential to good government. Moreover, the executive and legislative duties of the councillors, together with those of the many offices held by them, must have consumed a good deal of their time and left them without sufficient leisure to acquire that legal knowledge which they needed in the discharge of their judicial duties.

There was also the danger that the councillors might in certain contingencies be brought into an injudicial frame of mind by the performance of their military duties. Immediately after Bacon's rebellion, this potential evil developed into an abuse in actual practice. Some of the councillors, if not most of them, were opposed to the insurrectionary movement led by Bacon, and one of them, Ludwell, took the

---

" Robinson MSS., 28, 29. Virginia Court Book, 1623-1626, May, 1624.

In thus giving examples of penalties prescribed by the Quarter Court, no attempt is made to enumerate all the methods of punishment used by it. One other mode of correction employed by it might be mentioned; namely, that of binding offenders to service for certain lengths of time. The court in the early years could order a freeman to serve the colony for a term of years for violating certain regulations of the government. A runaway servant could be punished by lengthening his term of service and branding him with the letter " R." Robinson MSS., 11, 12, 76.

leading part in the war against the rebels.[75] After the rebellion was over, some of Bacon's followers were brought before the councillors, their enemies, for trial. The judges, or some of them at least, went into court with their war-spirit unabated, and were, therefore, not in a humor to deal fairly by their antagonists.[76]

And yet Bacon's followers would have fared much better than they did if all of them had been tried by the General Court, although its judges were their enemies. For if justice had been allowed to take its ordinary course, no death sentences would have been passed until after a jury had decided as to the guilt or innocence of the accused. But it was not the intention of the governor to allow juries to come between him and his revenge, and so he ordered the rebels to be tried by court martial without a jury.[77] By this means he was able to get many sentences of death against those who had taken part in the rebellion. According to the report of the King's commissioners, all who were tried by the court martial were sentenced to death and hanged, and so the accused were willing to accept any compromise rather than go to trial. When a person was brought before the court martial, he was asked whether he wished to be tried or to be fined at the discretion of the court without a trial, and the latter alternative was always preferred. A fine was then imposed upon him without the aid of a jury.[78] Berkeley's high-handed tyranny was not checked until the three commissioners appointed by the King to investigate conditions in the colony arrived in Virginia. On the arrival of these

[75] Neill, Virginia Carolorum, 360, 363, 364. Burk, History of Virginia, II, 180. General Court Records, 1670-1676, 247, 257.
[76] The commissioners sent over by the King to investigate conditions in Virginia reported that when they sat with the council on the trial of rebels, some of the loyalist party who sat with them were so unmindful of their position as judges that they railed at the prisoners from the bar as if they were the chief witnesses for the prosecution. Randolph MSS., 366. General Court Records, 1670-1676, 266, 267.
[77] Sainsbury MSS., 1676-1677, 118. Randolph MSS., 365. General Court Records, 1670-1676, 264-265.
[78] Randolph MSS., 366.

commissioners, trials by court martial ceased, and the General Court resumed its jurisdiction over criminal cases. After this no sentences of death were given against the rebels until after they had been indicted by a grand jury and tried by a petit jury.[79]

These acts of injustice committed against Bacon's followers were the greatest series of wrongs ever perpetrated in the name of the Virginia judiciary since the colony was freed from the military rule of Dale and Argoll. But the acquiescence of the court martial in the blood-thirsty demands of Berkeley is not to be taken as a proof that the governor's power was usually supreme in the administration of justice. Berkeley was, by a combination of unfortunate circumstances, raised to an eminence of power that the average governor never attained. The party of opposition had just been crushed, and was not able to make an effective protest against the arbitrary acts of the victor. Besides, many of the councillors were also opposed to the insurgent movement, and so there was in effect a union between the aristocracy and the King's representative against the conquered rebels. If the council, on this occasion, had stood out in manly opposition to the governor, as it frequently did at other times, this great stain on the ermine of Virginia would never have been made. We are glad to know, however, that the voice of protest was raised by the assembly against the atrocities practiced by the governor.[80]

Another flaw in the judicial system of Virginia was the entire exemption of the General Court from both direct and indirect responsibility to the people. As we have already seen, the people were not given a voice in the appointment or removal of councillors, and so to a greater extent than

---

[79] Randolph MSS., 365. General Court Records, 1670-76, 266, 267. In justice to Governor Berkeley, it ought to be said that an apologist for him claims that the death sentences passed by the court martial were all given in the heat of the rebellion at a time when he had no secure place in which to confine prisoners and no safe guard to keep them. Ibid., 372.

[80] Randolph MSS., 366.

was proper, the judges were relieved of the fear that they
would lose their places if they gave decisions that the people
considered unjust.   But the absence of this restraint on the
court left a dangerous power in the hands of the judges,
which they could employ towards the furtherance of their
own private ends.   There must ever have been before them
the temptation to give unfair decisions in those suits in which
they themselves or their friends were interested.[81]   Nor were
the councillors always strong enough to withstand this temptation.   In the last quarter of the seventeenth century, the
General Court fell into a practice by which each judge was
practically exempted from liability to all actions except those
that were brought with his own consent.   This abuse was
revealed to the Commissioners for Trade and Plantations by
an investigation which came in response to complaints of
certain English creditors made against the General Court
for withholding justice from them.   It was charged in these
complaints that a debt due them in Virginia could not be collected owing to the failure of the General Court to decide
suits brought against councillors.[82]

When the Commissioners inquired (1696) into the alleged
grievances, it discovered, to its great astonishment, that the

---

[81] It seems to have been the usual custom for a judge to leave
the bench whenever a suit to which he or his relatives were parties
came before the court for a hearing. But still it was to the interest of the judges to render a decision favorable to an absent col-
league, as they might want him to return the favor when they were
placed in the same situation. Spottswood's Letters, II, 60.

[82] However, these acts of injustice to foreigners did not of themselves mean necessarily that the court had fallen into extremely corrupt practices. The sense of public honor was not so high among
the Virginians of the seventeenth century as it is at present. This
is shown by the fact that during a considerable part of the seventeenth century the laws provided that the debts due to foreigners
by Virginians, except those contracted for imported goods, were not
recoverable in the Virginia courts. Nor was Virginia the only
colony that held lax views regarding obligations to foreigners. For
in 1731 we find British merchants making complaints against other
English colonies, saying that debts could not be collected in them.
We must, therefore, use the moral standards of the time in gauging
the degree of corruption involved in this discrimination against
foreigners. Hening, II, 189. Sainsbury MSS., 1606-1740, 108, 113,
115, 116; ibid., 1691-1697, 250.

General Court had a rule according to which an action could not be brought against any councillor without his consent. The practice of the court which had been in vogue for about sixteen years, was as follows:—When a suit was brought against a councillor, a notice of it was sent to him with the request that he appear before the court. If he failed to do so, the request was repeated, but no attachment was issued against his person or property to compel his attendance. By ignoring these notices, a councillor could postpone indefinitely the hearing of any suit against him. This indefinite postponement of cases was more unjust to the complainants than unfair decisions would have been because it deprived them of the privilege of appealing to the King. It was, therefore, left entirely optional with the councillors whether an action should ever be brought against them in the General Court.[83] This grievance, however, could be easily remedied, since all that was needed was a law providing that attachments be issued against the property of a councillor when he refused to appear in court to answer suits brought against him. Such a law was passed in 1705, and after this no mention of the abuse is found.[84]

It must not be inferred from this discussion of its weaknesses that the General Court was generally given to corrupt practices. In the documents that have been examined, only a few abuses are recorded, and this negative evidence goes far to show that the court usually gave the people a fair administration of justice.

COURTS OF OYER AND TERMINER.

After the sessions of the General Court were reduced to two a year, criminals were sometimes necessarily kept in prison six months before they could be tried. It was not long before the need for a more speedy administration of justice began to be felt, and this need led to the formation of a new criminal tribunal, the Court of Oyer and

---

[83] Sainsbury MSS., 1691-1697, 258, 259, 288, 331.
[84] Hening, III, 291, 292.

Terminer. The permanent establishment of this new court
dates from the first quarter of the eighteenth century, but
before this time special courts of oyer and terminer were
occasionally held in the colony. In the latter part of the
seventeenth century we find that the King sometimes sent
over special commissioners of oyer and terminer in which
certain persons were named as judges for the trial of particular cases.[85] But the King's order for convening these

---

[85] Sainsbury MSS., 1686-1688, 12; ibid., 1691-1697, 260; ibid., 1715-
1720, 698. Calendar of Virginia State Papers, I, 192.
  One of the most interesting and important cases that were tried
by special courts of oyer and terminer was that in which George
Talbot, a prominent citizen of Maryland, was arraigned for killing
Christopher Rousby, the King's collector of customs. The act was
committed on board *The Quaker,* a revenue vessel, which at that
time was lying in the harbor at the mouth of Patuxent Bay in
Maryland. The captain of the vessel was unwilling to deliver Talbot
up to the Maryland authorities, as he feared that they would not
punish him as he deserved. He, therefore, sailed to Virginia with
his captive and gave him over to Lord Howard, the governor. Lord
Howard thought that his commission as vice-admiral gave him authority to punish offenses of this class, and so Talbot was confined
in the jail of Gloucester County. The Maryland council wrote to
Governor Howard asking him to send Talbot back to Maryland for
trial, claiming that no other colony had jurisdiction in the case.
At a meeting of the Virginia council, which was called to consider
the matter, it was decided that all depositions should be sent to the
King for his opinion as to whether Talbot should be tried in Virginia according to the rules of admiralty or be sent to Maryland to
be tried according to common law. The Committee of Trade and
Plantations at first recommended that Talbot be sent to England for
trial, but afterwards decided that a special commission of oyer and
terminer should be sent to the council of Virginia for his trial.
The King also sent instructions to Lord Howard authorizing him to
suspend the execution of the sentence against Talbot if he should
be found guilty. But before this special court convened for his
trial, Talbot escaped from the Gloucester jail and returned to Maryland. Fiske says that he was liberated by his wife, who one dark,
wintry night sailed with two companions down the Chesapeake Bay
and up York River until they came to Gloucester. Talbot was delivered from prison and taken back to his home in Maryland. The
sheriff of Gloucester County and another prominent Virginian were
sent to Maryland for the prisoner, but it is not stated whether they
succeeded in bringing him back. At any rate, the case was put on
trial in Virginia before the General Court acting under a special
commission of oyer and terminer, and he was sentenced to death.
The King commuted the sentence (1686) to five years banishment
from the British dominions. Sainsbury MSS., 1682-1686, 134, 138, 142,
143, 146, 150, 162, 195, 209, 212; ibid., 1686-1688, 3, 12. Randolph
MSS., 426, 427. Fiske, Old Virginia and Her Neighbors, II, 158.

courts was not often given, and therefore, they were not an effective remedy against the delays in criminal trials. In 1692, an attempt was made to shorten the long intervals that came between the courts at which criminals could be tried. We find an order bearing date of that year which authorized the governor to grant special commissions of oyer and terminer at any time during the sessions of the General Court or assembly for the trial of capital offenses which could not be reported to the General Court on the day usually set for the hearing of criminal cases.[86]

Naturally, the next step to be taken in the development of the oyer and terminer courts was to introduce into these supplemental courts regularity as to the times of meeting. This step was attempted in 1710 when Lieutenant-Governor Spottswood was instructed by the Queen to require courts of oyer and terminer to be held regularly twice a year. Soon after his arrival, the governor called together his council and made known to them this order of the Queen. The councillors considered the innovation unnecessary, and replied that, in their opinion, criminal trials were already adequately provided for. There was, however, no important reason why they should object to the change, and when the governor again advised with them soon afterwards, they agreed to the new plan and recommended that the assembly provide for the expenses for carrying it out. The time set for the first meeting of the court was in December, 1710.[87]

The lieutenant-governor had thus succeeded in establishing regular courts of oyer and terminer without arousing the dangerous opposition of his council. If he had been satisfied to step here, it would have fared much better with him than it did. If he had not tried to use the new courts as a means of enlarging his own powers, this expansion of the judiciary could have taken place without occasioning any dispute over the new acquisition. But, unfortunately for him, he claimed, and two years later exercised the right of

---

[86] Calendar Virginia State Papers, I, 35, 36.
[87] Letters of Governor Spottswood, I, 8, 24.

naming in his commission of oyer and terminer persons other than councillors, which stirred up opposition against him in the council. The councillors regarded this as an attempt on the part of the governor to deprive them of their rights in the courts newly annexed to the judiciary. They did not, however, refuse to sit in the court of oyer and terminer the first time outsiders sat on the bench with them. Their reasons for yielding thus far in the beginning were that no criminal cases were tried at that particular court, and besides, they did not want their protest against the governor's action to take the form of a public affront. However, they asserted their right to act as sole judges in criminal trials, and the governor was soon convinced that they would not part with any of their judicial power without a struggle.[88]

The opposition of the council to this innovation led the governor to refer the question to the Lords of Trade for an opinion. The Lords of Trade decided that the governor did not have to confine himself entirely to councillors in choosing judges for the courts of oyer and terminer, unless such a limitation were imposed upon him by an act of the assembly.[89] Spottswood thought that his opponents would acquiesce in this decision, and in 1717 he named as judges of a court of oyer and terminer five councillors and four other prominent men. These outsiders were added, according to his own statement, to show the people that the power of the crown over the judiciary was the same in Virginia as it was in England. Some of the councillors were still unwilling to concede the governor's right to create judges in this way, and so refused to sit in this court.[90] Eight members of the council declared that they would not act as judges in these courts if any persons other than councillors were appointed to sit with them.[91] The dispute, therefore, continued open,

[88] Byrd MSS., II, 199-202. Spottswood's Letters, II, 25-26.
[89] Sainsbury MSS., 1715-1720, 521, 522.
[90] Ibid., 637. Spottswood's Letters, II, 26, 259, 260.
[91] Sainsbury MSS., 1715-1720, 578.

and much bitterness of feeling was engendered before a final settlement was reached.

Prominent among the leaders of the opposition were Commissary Blair, Philip Ludwell, and William Byrd, all men of great influence in the colony. Byrd sent a remonstrance to the Lords Commissioners of Trade and Plantations, in which he brought forth able arguments to show that the governor could not go outside of the council in selecting judges. The innovation, he said, was a violation of the laws and chartered privileges of the colony. Besides, it gave the governor an undue influence over these courts, and, therefore, left the lives and fortunes of the people too much at his mercy. For the judges of the oyer and terminer courts were appointed, not for life or for a certain number of years, but for one term of the court. If the governor, therefore, wished to punish any one, he could at each term of the court appoint as judges such men as would vote for the sentence he desired.[92] Spottswood replied to these objections, and pointed out that there were precedents in favor of the practice inaugurated by him. The King, he said, had sometimes joined others with councillors in his special commissions of oyer and terminer, and in the slave courts justices of the peace gave the death sentence. He also declared that the judges whom he had appointed to sit with the councillors in these courts were as well qualified to try criminals as the councillors themselves.[93]

But before the governor sent in his reply to Byrd, the contest had reached a stage in which an important constitutional question was involved. In order that the mooted point might be settled once for all, the Lords of Trade appealed to the attorney-general of England for his opinion on them. The attorney-general decided that the governor had not infringed any legal provision by the exercise of the disputed power, but recommended that he be restrained from

---

[92] Calendar of Va. State Papers, I, 190-193. Sainsbury MSS., 1715-1720, 578, 708.
[93] Sainsbury MSS., 1715-1720, 698-701.

convening these courts except on " extraordinary emergencies." In January, 1718, the Lords of Trade sent this opinion to the governor and intimated that he was expected to act in accordance with the recommendation coupled with it.[94]

The assembly now came forward to champion the cause of the council. In May, 1718, it sent a petition to the King asking that the councillors might be the sole judges of the courts of oyer and terminer, or that His Majesty would in some other way restrain this dangerous power of the governor. But the Lords of Trade refused to grant this request, and the council gave up its attempt to exclude outsiders from the bench of the oyer and terminer courts.[95]

In the settlement of the dispute neither the governor nor the council could claim a complete victory. The governor had gained his point in so far as his power to appoint other judges to sit with the councillors in the oyer and terminer courts had been upheld; but the Lords of Trade had to forego most of the fruits of the victory as they receded from their first position. According to the instructions first given to Spottswood, these courts were to be held regularly twice a year, but he was now advised to convene them only on very important occasions.[96] The failure of the council to obtain from the Board a theoretical recognition of their right to act as sole judges in the courts of oyer and terminer seems to have been only a nominal defeat. For in the first court of oyer and terminer that was held after the councillors yielded, no outsiders were appointed to sit with them as judges.[97] Then, too, the immediate successor of Spottswood, Hugh Drysdale, seems to have profited by Spottswood's experience and to have prudently abstained from antagonizing his council by exercising the disputed power.

[94] Sainsbury MSS., 1715-1720, 669, 675, 676, 686.
[95] Ibid., 740, 770. Spottswood's Letters, II, 321.
[96] Sainsbury MSS., 1715-1720, 675, 676, 678. Randolph MSS., 498. Spottswood's Letters, I, 8.
[97] Spottswood's Letters, II, 321.

Before the end of the first year of his administration, the council had unanimously agreed that the courts of oyer and terminer should be regularly held according to the King's instructions.[98] Now we can hardly believe that those men who had contended so strenuously for their rights during Spottswood's administration [99] would now consent to the formation of a regular tribunal unless they felt assured that they would always be chosen as its sole judges. At any rate, there is no doubt that by the middle of the eighteenth century (1755), it was customary for the oyer and terminer courts to be composed exclusively of councillors.[100] We may, therefore, safely say that the councillors eventually won all that they were contending for, and that the victory of the governor and Lords of Trade was an empty one, which barely enabled them to come out of the contest with their dignity unimpaired.

The fact that the council was able to push its opposition to such a successful issue argues much for the influence wielded by it in the colony. The power possessed by the councillors at this particular period was greater than that usually enjoyed by them, and Spottswood ought to have seen that during his administration the time was most inopportune for a governor to measure lances with them. Seven of them, more than a majority, were related,[101] and it was, therefore, easy for them to combine against the crown representative. Besides, the family to which most of the councillors belonged had already procured the removal of two governors, which emboldened them against Spottswood and made them popular with the people.[102] On the other hand, Spottswood's power was weakened by the opposition which the assembly was waging against him.[103] The council's success in this

---

[98] Sainsbury MSS., 1720-1730, 74, 75.
[99] Spottswood's council was passed on to Drysdale with few, if any, changes in its personnel. Ibid., 1715-1720, 578, 593. Council Journal, 1721-1734, 3, 11, 16, 27, 32-34.
[100] Dinwiddie Papers, I, 384.
[101] Spottswood's Letters, II, 60.
[102] Sainsbury MSS., 1715-1720, 709.
[103] Ibid., 740. Southern Literary Mesenger, XVII, 590-592.

quarrel was also doubtless due, in large measure, to the able leadership of Commissary Blair and Colonel William Byrd.

This dispute was a struggle directly between the council and the King's representative, but indirectly a contest between the colonial government and the crown. The council was supported by the representatives of the people,[104] and the governor, by the Lords of Trade, for this board saw in the council's objections to the innovation only a desire to conserve its own authority at the expense of the King's power.[105]

It is difficult to determine what support the people gave the aristocracy in their brave struggle with the King's representative. It would seem that they were not indifferent to this increase of the governor's authority, as their representatives, the Burgesses, expressed their disapproval of it. But Spottswood says that the Burgesses at this time were much in disfavor with the people;[106] and if this be true, their address in support of the council cannot be taken as an expression of popular opinion. He also claimed that the people refused to concern themselves with the council's quarrel. According to his account, a paper was drawn up in the form of a grievance against the oyer and terminer courts, and was sent out to the counties to be signed by the citizens. But despite this attempt to work up sentiment against the governor's action, only two counties sent in grievances against these courts, and one of these remonstrances had only eighteen signatures and the other only eleven.[107]

It might at first thought appear that this protest of the councillors was only an expression of that factious spirit which they too often betrayed during this period.[108] But if the innovation attempted by the governor had been carried out without opposition, it would in all probability have materially altered the relation of the colony to the mother

---

[104] Sainsbury MSS., 1715-1720, 740.
[105] Ibid., 691.
[106] Ibid., 779.
[107] Ibid., 706. Spottswood's Letters, II, 276.
[108] Campbell, History of Virginia, 398.

country. The proposed change would have meant a transfer of a certain amount of power from the Virginia aristocracy to the King's representative, and through him to the King himself, and, therefore, the colony would to that extent have been deprived of its local autonomy. Besides, this transfer of power could not have been effected without giving the governor a dangerous influence over the judiciary. This new privilege of the executive was, as Colonel Byrd pointed out, liable to great abuse. It is true that Spottswood did not use the new courts as a means of procuring unjust sentences against his enemies, for he did not require any criminals to be tried in them who desired to wait for the regular sessions of the General Court.[109] But the opposition of the council was aimed not so much at Spottswood's policy as at the principle underlying that policy.[110] If no voice of protest had been raised at this time against executive aggression, the new power would have been confirmed to the King's representative by precedent. There would always have been present the danger that an able and unscrupulous governor would use his influence over the judiciary as a means of gratifying his private spite. The council, therefore, did the colony a great service by thus resisting this encroachment upon its privileges. It may be true that the councillors, as was charged by the Lords of Trade, made the fight to protect their own interests rather than to protect the rights of the people.[111] But their service to Virginia was none the less valuable because it was not performed entirely for altruistic reasons. For it seems that colonial Virginia owes the absence of this element of despotism from her constitution to the stand which the council at this time made against the governor's attempted aggression.

However, the strife over the oyer and terminer court ceased in a few years,[112] and the new tribunal became a per-

---

[109] Sainsbury MSS., 1715-1720, 796.
[110] Ibid., 69. Spottswood's Letters, II, 26, 222.
[111] Sainsbury MSS., 1715-1720, 691.
[112] Spottswood's Letters, II, 341.

manent part of the Virginia judiciary. After the court had
become established, its sessions were held twice a year,
in June and December, and the intervals between the terms
of the General Court were thus equally divided.[113]

In both the General Court and the oyer and terminer
courts, important criminal offenses were tried by a petit
jury after indictments had been made by the grand jury.[114]

It has already been shown that the right to be tried by
a jury of their compeers was one of the privileges that the
first settlers brought with them from England.[115] · This right
was called into exercise for the first time in 1607 in the
trial of two suits for slander brought by John Smith and
John Robinson against Edward Maria Wingfield, the first
president of the local council.[116] Juries were several times
called on to decide causes during the few years in which
Virginia was under the first charter that was granted to
the Company.[117] In Dale's scheme of military government
there was no provision for juries, and they probably had no
place in the martial courts that dealt out summary punishment to offenders. But after this military tyranny had
given place to the régime of freedom inaugurated by Yeardley, the people began again to enjoy the right of trial by
jury, and as early as 1625 we find the governor and council
making use of this privilege.[118]

According to the usual custom the grand jury of the General Court was selected from the freeholders who happened
to be at the capital while the court was in session.[119] For the

---

[113] Virginia Gazette, Dec. 15, 1768; June 15, 1769. Webb, Virginia Justice, 107. Hugh Jones, Present State of Virginia, 29.
[114] Robinson MSS., 75, 76, 83. General Court Records, 1670-1676,
8, 20, 53, 154, 235. Hening, IV, 403; V, 543.
[115] See page 11.
[116] Wingfield's True Discourse, published in Arber's Works of
Smith, LXXXIII. In Winsor's Narrative and Critical History of
America (Vol. III, p. 146) it is erroneously stated that the first
trial by jury in Virginia was in 1630, when ex-Govenor Pott was
arraigned before the Quarter Court for cattle stealing.
[117] Arber, Works of Smith, 12, 13.
[118] Virginia Court Book, 1623-1626, August, 1623.
[119] Randolph MSS., 412. Hening, V, 524, 525. Mercer, Virginia
Laws, 160. Webb, Virginia Justice, 198.

grand jury of the oyer and terminer court, the sheriffs of James City and York Counties [120] each had to summon twelve men to come before the court. A grand jury of not less than fifteen was to be sworn out of those that obeyed the summons.[121]

The petit jury in both courts was usually composed of twelve men, though in the early records of the General Court, panels of thirteen, fourteen, and twenty-four are mentioned.[122] The English custom of trying criminals by juries of the vicinage could not be followed by the General Court without great inconvenience and expense. But in 1662, a law was passed providing for the partial adoption of this practice by the General Court. According to this statute, every crime punishable by loss of life or member was to be tried by a jury of twelve men, six of whom were to be selected from bystanders and six were to be summoned from the vicinity in which the crime was committed.[123] This method of choosing jurors was employed by the General Court for nearly three-quarters of a century.[124]

When the court of oyer and terminer was established, criminals brought before it were tried by a jury of twelve men from the county in which the crime had been committed, according to the common law of England. In 1734, the practice in both courts was made uniform by a law which provided that twelve men of the vicinage should be summoned whenever an important criminal case was to be tried by either court. The places of those who were challenged or who failed to appear were to be filled with bystanders.[125] But this method was found inconvenient and expensive.

---

[120] Williamsburg, the capital, was on the border of these two counties, being partly in both.

[121] Hening, IV, 403; V, 543. Mercer, Va. Laws, 160. Webb, Va. Justice, 199.

[122] Robinson MSS., 75. Hening, I, 145, 146.

[123] Hening, II, 63, 64.

[124] Hartwell, Blair, and Chilton, 47. Calendar Virginia State Papers, I, 8, 34, 35. Hening, IV, 404. Beverley, Book IV, p. 23.

[125] Hening, IV, 403, 404; V, 544. Mercer, Virginia Laws, 218. Webb, Virginia Justice, 199.

Besides, it was noticed that most of the sentences given for
capital offenses were against those persons who had been
convicted of crimes in Great Britain or Ireland before
they were brought to Virginia. It was held that no advantage could come to such persons from being tried by a jury
of the vicinage, as they were generally not known even in
the county in which they lived. It was, therefore, enacted
in 1738, that in trials for capital crimes, juries should be
made up of bystanders in all cases in which the accused was
still serving a term for a crime committed in Great Britain
or Ireland.[126] Juries of bystanders were also usually employed by the General Court in the determination of civil
causes and in the trial of minor criminal offenses.[127] The
property qualification for jury service in the General Court
and the courts of oyer and terminer was fixed by laws of the
eighteenth century at one hundred pounds sterling.[128]

During the colonial period, the severity of the laws was
mitigated by the custom of allowing the benefit of clergy
to criminals. According to the ancient practice in England,
those who were entitled to this privilege could claim it in
all cases of petit treason and in most cases of capital felonies.
Before Virginia was settled, English statutes had added
certain other offenses to this list of exceptions. This raised
the question as to whether the class of criminals thus excepted by Parliament were to be excluded from the benefit
of clergy in Virginia. The opinion generally held was that
clergy should not be allowed in Virginia in those cases in
which it had been taken away by these English statutes;
but as doubt might arise on this point, the assembly in
1732 reviewed the question and declared in favor of the com-
monly accepted view.

For a long time the benefit of clergy was not granted in

---

[126] Hening, V, 24, 25, 545. Mercer, Virginia Laws, 57, 58.
[127] Hening, III, 369; V, 525. Mercer, Virginia Laws, 217. Beverley, Book IV, p. 22. Hening, II, 73, 74. Hartwell, Blair, and Chilton, 47. Hammond, Leah, and Rachel, published in Force's Tracts,
p. 16. General Court Records, 1670-1676, 150, 158.
[128] Hening, III, 176, 370; V, 525. Mercer, Va. Laws, 218, 219.

England to laymen under the rank of peers unless they could read, but in the fifth year of Queen Anne's reign a law was passed by Parliament which did away with this unjust discrimination against laymen. In 1732, the Virginia assembly, following this precedent, extended the benefit of clergy to negroes, Indians, and mulattoes, and ordered that the reading test should thereafter never be required of anyone who should claim this privilege.[129]

In the list of crimes which were placed without the benefit of clergy by the statutes were murder, burglary, burning of houses, horse stealing, and man-slaughter when committed by a negro, Indian or mulatto. Also if a negro, Indian, or mulatto was convicted of breaking into a house in the daytime and stealing as much as five (afterwards twenty) shillings, he was to be punished without benefit of clergy. Clergy was allowed to a criminal only once during his lifetime.[130]

When the court granted the benefit of clergy to an offender, it substituted burning in the hand for the death penalty.[131] According to Starke, the old English custom required that the letter " M " be branded in the hand of murderers and " T " in that of other felons. This imprint was burnt into the hand not merely to punish the criminal, but also to put a mark on him which would show that he had received the benefit of clergy and thus keep him from deceiving the court into granting the privilege a second time.[132] But in the eighteenth century branding seems to have been regarded as a mere act of form in Virginia, for it could be done with a cold iron.[133] When a person was

---

[129] Hening, IV, 325, 326. Mercer, 54. One case is given in which the General Court of Virginia required reading before allowing clergy. General Court Records, 1670-1676, 53. Blackstone's Commentaries, IV, 296, 299.

[130] Hening, IV, 326. Webb, Virginia Justice, 82, 83. Starke, Virginia Justice, 87. Mercer, Virginia Laws, 54.

[131] Webb, Virginia Justice, 83. Virginia Gazette, Oct. 29, 1736; June 10, Oct. 28, 1737; May 12, Dec. 15, 1768; June 15, 1769.

[132] Starke, Va. Justice, 87. Blackstone, IV, 294.

[133] Virginia Gazette, Dec. 7, 1739. Starke, 88.

admitted to clergy, he forfeited all his goods, but when he
was burnt in the hand, he was reinstated in the posses-
sion of his lands. By the act of branding, his credit was
also restored, and his disability for acting as a witness was
removed.[134] Indians, negroes, and mulattoes, who were given
the benefit of clergy, besides being burnt in the hand, could
be punished by whipping.[135]

ECCLESIASTICAL AND ADMIRALTY COURTS.

There was one independent ecclesiastical court in the
colony, which was held by the Commissary of the Bishop of
London, though it was not a court in the true sense of the
term. The immoralities of the clergy were the only offenses
of which it took cognizance and deprivation of, and suspension from, office were the only punishments which it could
impose. From this court appeals could be taken to the
Court of Delegates in England.[136] This was a narrower
jurisdiction than that exercised by the ecclesiastical courts
of England during the colonial period. The other spiritual
causes which were cognizable in the English ecclesiastical
courts were determined in Virginia by the regular common
law courts.[137] In England matrimonial and testamentary
causes were tried by the spiritual courts; while in Virginia,
they were heard by the regular common law courts. As has
already been shown, the General Court and the county courts
examined wills and gave certificates thereon, and the governor signed the orders for executing them.[138] No record of
absolute divorces has been found, and apparently they were
not often given during the colonial period. However, divorces *a mensa et thoro* were granted by both the General
Court and the county courts, and a marriage could be

---

[134] Starke, 91. Blackstone, IV, 300.

[135] Mercer, 54.

[136] Dinwiddie Papers, I, 384.

[137] Hartwell, Blair, and Chilton, 49, 50. Webb, Virginia Justice,
206. Blackstone, III, 87-97.

[138] See page 45. Blackstone, edited by Chitty, III, pp. 67-73. Beverley, History of Va., Book IV, p. 21.

annulled *ab initio* by the General Court if the contracting
parties were within " the Levitical degrees prohibited by the
laws of England." [139]

During the greater part of the seventeenth century, there
was no need of a separate court of admiralty in Virginia.
In a report sent to England in 1671, Governor Berkeley
said that it had been twenty-eight years since a prize had
been brought into the colony.[140] The few maritime causes
that came up for a hearing were determined by the regular
courts, which could employ juries to assist them in rendering decisions.[141] This method of trial must have been unfavorable to a strict enforcement of the navigation laws, for
both judges and juries would naturally be disinclined to give
severe sentences for violations of laws that they considered
unjust to the colony. The theory that the courts dealt leniently with smugglers is supported by the fact that the home
government at the end of the century felt called upon to
establish a court of vice-admiralty in the colony. An order
for erecting a court of admiralty in Virginia appears in
the instructions given to Lord Howard in 1690.[142] But this
order seems not to have been complied with by him, and it
was renewed to Governor Andros in 1697. The council
had already expressed its approval of the plan, and next
year Andros established a court of vice-admiralty, whose

---

[139] Calendar Virginia State Papers, 29. General Court Records,
1670-1676, 262. Robinson MSS., 16, 75. Elizabeth City County Court
Records, 1684-1699, 235. Virginia Magazine of History and Biography, I, 40; VIII, 175. Hening, IV, 245-246.
According to the Rev. Hugh Jones, the ecclesiastical courts of
Virginia were in his day very unpopular with the people and their
very name was hateful to them. But it must be borne in mind that
Hugh Jones's views were narrow and biased, and it is, therefore,
not improbable that he construed the opposition of a certain faction
of the clergy to the Commissary's reforms into a general discontent
of the people with the practices of the spiritual courts. Hugh Jones,
Present State of Virginia, 66.
[140] Chalmers, Political Annals, 325.
[141] Virginia Magazine of History and Biography, V, 38; XII, 189.
Hening, I, 466, 467, 537, 538. General Court Records, 1670-1676, 8,
40, 41, 42, 253. Beverley, History of Va., Book IV, pp. 20, 21.
Hartwell, Blair, and Chilton, 43.
[142] Sainsbury MSS., 1640-1691, 334.

territorial jurisdiction was to embrace Virginia and North Carolina.[143]

The establishment of the colonial courts of vice-admiralty was, in a sense, an extension of the jurisdiction of the High Court of Admiralty to the colonies.[144] At first the judge was appointed by the governor, but later the judge was commissioned by the High Court of Admiralty of Great Britain, and the other officers—the advocate, the marshal, and the register—were chosen by the governor.[145] The court took cognizance of violations of the trade and quarantine laws and other maritime causes, except that it did not have jurisdiction over offenses committed on the King's ships of war. Appeals from decisions given by this court could be made to the High Court of Admiralty in England or to the King in council.[146]

The governor took a prominent part in admiralty proceedings. He was vice-admiral of the colony, and had power to appoint masters of vessels and grant them commissions to execute martial law.[147] The courts of vice-admiralty were not convened at regular intervals but were called only when there were cases to be tried.[148] The court as constituted in 1736 was composed of not less than seven judges, one of whom was always either the governor, or the lieutenant-governor, or a councillor. Merchants, planters, factors and officers of ships were also eligible to a seat on the bench of this court.[149]

---

[143] Sainsbury MSS., 1691-1697, 292, 315. Ibid., 1706-1714, 323. William and Mary College Quarterly, V, 129.
Just how long this court continued to hear maritime causes coming up from North Carolina, I am unable to say.
[144] Blackstone, III, 69.
[145] Dinwiddie Papers, I, 384. William and Mary College Quarterly, V, 129.
[146] Dinwiddie Papers, I, 384. Hening, III, 178; IV, 99-101; ibid., 1691-1697, 135, 137. Blackstone, ed. by Chitty, III, p. 54.
[147] Sainsbury MSS., 1625-1715, 55; ibid., 1640-1691, 334; ibid., 1705-1707, 58, 526. Dinwiddie Papers, I, 384. Beverley, Hist. of Va., Book IV, p. 4. Hartwell, Blair, and Chilton, 20.
[148] Dinwiddie Papers, I, 384. Blackstone, III, 68.
[149] Webb, Virginia Justice, 107, 249, 250. Virginia Gazette, Sept. 15, 1738.

The methods employed in dealing out punishment for piracy were not uniform. In 1687, the King appointed a special commissioner to supervise the trial of pirates in Virginia.[150] Ten years later the English method of inquiring into and punishing offenses committed at sea was adopted in the colony. According to a law enacted in 1699, all piracies, treasons, felonies and other crimes committed on the high seas, or in the bays, harbors or rivers under the jurisdiction of the admiral[151] were to be tried by a special court of oyer and terminer called for that purpose. The judge of the court of vice-admiraly and " such other substantial persons " as the governor should see fit were to be the judges of this court.[152] In the early part of the eighteenth century, commissioners were appointed by the Queen to try pirates in Virginia and North Carolina. According to Webb, whose work was published in 1736, it was the custom in his day for the commissioners appointed by the King, or some of them at least, to sit in the court of vice-admiralty, before which persons charged with piracy were brought for trial.[153]

---

[150] Sainsbury MSS., 1686-1688, 88, 144; ibid., 1625-1715, 142.

[151] The term admiral was used here to designate the governor, who was vice-admiral of the colony.

[152] Hening, III, 178. Statutes of the Realm, 28, Henry VIII, C. 15. Hugh Jones, Present State of Virginia, 29.

[153] Webb, Virginia Justice, 107. Sainsbury MSS., 1705-1707, 30; ibid., 1715-1720, 779, 780.

CHAPTER III.

THE INFERIOR COURTS.

The Monthly or County Courts.—The most important inferior court was the one regularly held in each county. It was at first known as the monthly court, but it was afterwards given the English name of county court. The first monthly courts were established as early as 1624. At that time it was provided by an act of assembly that courts should be held every month in the corporations of Charles City and Elizabeth City.[1]

The creation of these courts was the necessary outcome of the rapid growth of the colony which began in 1619. When the cleared areas began to lengthen along the river and to encroach more and more on the wilderness, it became very inconvenient for those colonists living at a distance from James City to go there for the arbitration of their minor differences. The need of local adjudication in small matters naturally became felt first in the more remote settlements, and, as one would expect, the first two monthly courts were established on the eastern and western frontiers. The jurisdiction of the county courts was limited to petty cases coming up from the precincts immediately adjacent to them, and thus the judicial authority of the governor and council was, for a considerable part of the country, left unimpaired.

---

[1] In an address made before the Virginia Bar Association in 1894, Judge Waller Staples said that monthly courts were first established in 1623. This statement is based on a law passed by the assembly in 1624; the mistake in the date arises, I presume, from an erroneous reading of " 1623-4," which is given by Hening as the date of the act.

It is not improbable that these two courts were established as early as the year 1619, and that the act of 1624 was only a statutory recognition of what had already been accomplished in fact. Hening, I, 125. Proceedings Virginia State Bar Association, Vol. VII, 129. McDonald Papers, I, 137.

It was not long before the growth of the colony demanded an extension of this branch of the judiciary. By 1632, three other monthly courts had been created, one of which was located on the eastern side of the Chesapeake Bay.[2] In 1634, the colony was divided into eight shires, corresponding to the shires of England, in each of which a court was to be held every month.[3] Other counties were formed from time to time, and each one was given a local court as soon as it was organized. In 1658, there were sixteen counties in Virginia;[4] in 1671, twenty;[5] in 1699, twenty-two;[6] in 1714, twenty-five;[7] and by 1782, the number had increased to seventy-four.[8]

By the act of 1624, it was provided that the judges of the monthly courts should be "the commanders of the places and such others as the governor and council shall appoint by commission."[9] The judges were at first known as commissioners of the monthly courts, but were afterwards given the title of justice of the peace.[10] The office of justice of the peace was one of dignity, and was generally held by men of influence and ability.[11] Apparently few of the magistrates were learned in the law, and many of them probably had little general education.[12] But the causes determined by the

---

[2] Hening, I, 168.
[3] Hening, I, 224.
[4] Ibid., 424-431.
[5] Ibid., II, 511, 512.
[6] Virginia Magazine of History and Biography, I, 230-236.
[7] Ibid., II, 3-15.
[8] Jefferson's Notes on Virginia, 116.
[9] Hening, I, 125.
[10] Hening, I, 132, 133; ibid., II, 70.
[11] Hening, II, 69. Council Journal, 1721-1734, 219. Spottswood's Letters, II, 193. Calendar Va. State Papers, I, 88.
[12] According to an interesting account written by Hartwell, Blair, and Chilton about the end of the seventeenth century, the justices of the peace in their day were less qualified for the duties of their office than were those chosen in the early years. The reason for this, they said, was that the first settlers, having been reared in England, had had better opportunities for acquiring a knowledge of the common law than the Virginians of a later period, who had been brought up in the colony where there were few educational advantages. Hartwell, Blair, and Chilton, 44.

county courts did not, as a rule, involve difficult points of law, and, therefore, the sound judgment and good common sense of the justices must in a large measure have compensated for their lack of legal knowledge.

The judges of the monthly courts were at first appointed by the governor and council.[13]   In the beginning of the Commonwealth period, the Burgesses and the commissioners sent to Virginia by Parliament ordered that the commissioners of the county courts should be chosen by the House of Burgesses.[14]   But this provision was repealed the next year (1653), when the governor and council were given power to appoint commissioners on the recommendation of the county courts.[15]   In 1658, it was enacted that appointments so made should be confirmed by the assembly.[16]   The method of selecting judges that was employed during the Commonwealth period did not go far towards bringing the county courts into responsibility to the people; for, with the exception of the first year, it gave the people little, if any, control over the appointment of their commissioners.   The Puritan Revolution, therefore, did not go far towards democratizing the lower branch of the Virginia judiciary.

From the Restoration to the end of the colonial period, county justices were commissioned by the governors, though they were often, if not generally, appointed with the advice and consent of the council.[17]   Justices were not chosen for any definite period of time, and it seems that their commissions could be renewed at the discretion of the governor. But most, if not all, of the old members were usually named

---

[13] Hening, I, 125. Accomac County Court Records, 1632-1640, 9. Lower Norfolk County Records, 1637-1643, 159.
[14] Hening, I, 372.
[15] Ibid., 376, 402.
[16] Ibid., 480.
[17] Council Journal, 1721-1734, 219, 286. Essex County Court Records, 1683-1686, 153. Henrico County Court Records, 1677-1692, I, 133, 134, 244; ibid, 1710-1714, 253. Warwick County Court Records, 1748-1762, 42, 155. Hening, II, 69, 70. Calendar Virginia State Papers, I, 16, 191. Sainsbury MSS., 1691-1697, 335. Spottswood's Letters, II, 193. Dinwiddie Papers, I, 383.

in the new commissions, and so the appointments were practically made for life.[18] It does not appear whether the practice of filling vacancies in the county commissions on the
recommendation of the county courts was discontinued
immediately after the Restoration, but if it was, it was
afterwards revived. For in the later years we find the
justices claiming and exercising the right of making nominations for vacancies in their respective courts.[19] This custom made the county courts self-perpetuating bodies, and
rendered them practically independent of the executive.

The number of justices appointed for the county courts
varied at different times and in different counties, but usually
ranged from about eight to eighteen.[20] But the justices were

---

[18] Henrico County Court Records, 1677-1692, 133, 244, 271, 373;
ibid., 1737-1746, 374. Richmond County Court Records, 1692-1694,
102. Sainsbury MSS., 1625-1715, 65. Hartwell, Blair, and Chilton,
43. Rappahannock County Records, 1686-1692, 203, 207, 209, 211,
213, 218. Warwick County Records, 1748-1762, 38, 47, 49, 53, 57.

[19] Council Journal, 1721-1743, 43, 262, 311. Rappahannock County
Court Records, 1686-1692, 190. Henrico County Court Records,
1737-1746, 339. Warwick County Records, 1748-1762, 42, 155.
We do not find any law compelling the governor to appoint the
nominees of the county courts, but it was good policy for him to
do so. For if he were to choose as new justices men who were not
acceptable to the old ones, it would be liable to stir up opposition
against him in the counties. That the justices were jealous of their
power to nominate to vacancies is evident from the action taken by
the court of Spottsylvania County in 1744 when this privilege was
infringed by the governor. Three new justices were put in the commission of Spottsylvania County who had not been recommended by
the court. Some of the old justices regarded this as an affront to
them, and seven of them refused to sit on the bench. Calendar
Virginia State Papers, I, 238.

[20] In one of the commissions granted in 1632, only five names are
mentioned. In 1642, eleven commissioners were appointed for Accomac County, and eight were put in the commission given to
Lower Norfolk County in the same year. In 1661 a law was passed
by the assembly restricting the number to eight for each county. In
1699 the average number of justices for all the counties was about
twelve; in 1714, a little more than fourteen. Hening, I, 169; II, 21.
Accomac County Court Records, 1640-1645, 148. Lower Norfolk
County Records, 1637-1643, 159. Sainsbury MSS., 1691-1697, 335.
Mercer, Virginia Laws, 62. Henrico County Records, 1677-1692,
244, 332; ibid., 1719-1724, 6; ibid., 1710-1714, 253-309. Rappahannock County Records, 1686-1692, 211. Charles City County Records, 1758-1762, 246. Warwick County Records, 1748-1762, 57.
Winder MSS., I, 203. Virginia Magazine of History and Biography,
I, 230-236, 364-373; II, 3-15.

very irregular in their attendance at courts, and, as a rule, more than one-half of them were absent at every session.[21] The court could not convene for the transaction of business unless as many as four justices were present.[22] It sometimes happened that courts could not be held at the appointed times because there were not enough judges present to make a quorum. This caused considerable inconvenience to witnesses and parties to suits, especially if they lived at considerable distances from the county-seats. This irregularity in the meeting of the courts was complained of from time to time, and attempts were made to compel a more regular attendance of the judges. Laws were passed providing for fines to be imposed on all justices who should be absent from the court sessions without a good excuse. But despite these measures, the county courts continued to be poorly attended by the magistrates during the entire colonial period.[23]

Long before Virginia was settled, there had grown up in the county court system of England the practice of appoint-

---

[21] The following facts regarding the average attendance of justices at courts have been gathered from the court records of the counties mentioned below. The average attendance for Lower Norfolk County from 1638 to 1640 was about five; for Accomac from 1640 to 1645, five; for York from 1672 to 1676, little more than five; for Rappahannock from 1686 to 1692, between four and five; for Henrico from 1738 to 1740, between four and five; for Charles City from 1761 to 1762, about five.

[22] Lower Norfolk County Records, 1637-1643, 159. Henrico Records, 1677-1692, I, 244. Winder MS., I, 204. Sainsbury MSS., 1691-1697, 335.

When the monthly courts were first organized, three commissioners constituted a quorum. Hening, I, 133.

[23] It is probable that these provisions were not strictly enforced, as the fines for absences were to be imposed by the county courts. One would naturally expect the justices to deal leniently with their colleagues for staying away from the meetings of the courts when they, themselves, were often guilty of the same offense. It was doubtless this failure on the part of the county courts to punish delinquences in attendance that caused Governor Spottswood, in 1711, to order the sheriffs to report all excuses for absences to him. However, it does not appear whether Governor Spottswood's plan was a more effective remedy for the evil than were the measures adopted by the assembly. Hening, I, 350, 454; II, 70, 71. Henrico County Records, 1710-1714, 56, 57. Warwick County Records, 1748-1762, 86, 92. Winder MSS., II, 171.

ing certain justices of the peace to be of the quorum. By this was meant that no court could be legally held unless one of them was present. This custom probably owed its origin to the ignorance of the justices in matters of law. Judicial skill was not to be expected of every country squire; consequently, it was necessary to appoint certain ones " eminent for their skill and discretion " to be of the quorum and to order that no court should be held in which the salutary advice of at least one of them could not be felt.[24] Upon the organization of the monthly courts, this same practice was adopted in Virginia. Whenever a commission was given to the justices of a county, certain of them were mentioned by name as belonging to the quorum. One, at least, of the persons so designated had to be present at every court, else no causes could be tried. The number of the quorum varied from time to time, and in the different counties, and generally increased as the county courts grew in importance.[25]

Prior to 1643, the statutes ordered that the local courts should be held every month, and, therefore, they were called monthly courts. At this time it was enacted that they should meet once in two months, and the term county court was substituted for the old name.[26] By the end of the seventeenth century the custom of meeting monthly had been revived, and was kept up from that time until the end of the colonial period.[27]

The place where justice was administered was usually some conveniently located hamlet or village, which might be

---

[24] Cooley's Blackstone, I, 349-350.

[25] Hening, I, 125, 133. Accomac County Records, 1640-1645, 148. Surry Records, 1645-1672, 359-360. Lower Norfolk County Records, 1637-1643, 159. Virginia Magazine of History and Biography, I, 230-236; II, 3-15. Henrico County Records, 1677-1692, 134.

[26] Hening, I, 272, 273, 462. Hammond, Leah and Rachel, 15, 16. Winder MSS., I, 204. Henrico Records, 1677-1692, 134; ibid., 1697-1704, 165, 301. Rappahannock Records, 1686-1692, 4-252.

[27] Hening, III, 504; V, 489. Henrico Records, 1710-1714, 38, 42, 80, 91, 92; ibid., 1719-1724, 23, 27, 33, 39; ibid., 1737-1746, 15, 22, 28, 34. Charles City County Records, 1758-1762, 87, 99, 103, 106, 115. Beverley, History of Va., Book IV, p. 24. Hartwell, Blair, and Chilton, 43. Mercer, Va. Laws, 62.

called the county-seat. In the early years, however, we find
that in one or two of the counties, the sessions of the courts
were frequently held at the houses of the commissioners.
In such cases, the courts generally journeyed from the home
of one commissioner to that of another, and thus all the
magistrates shared equally the burden of entertaining their
colleagues.[28] Sometimes when a county was divided by a
large stream, two court-houses were erected, one on each
side of the river, and the courts were held in both.[29]

The jurisdiction of the county courts extended to both
civil and criminal cases.[30] Chancery causes were also cognizable in them, and the justices were required to take separate oaths as judges in chancery.[31] Once a year, at least, the
justices held an orphans' court, which inquired into the
management of the estates of orphans and bound out father-
less children who had no property. It was also the business
of this court to see that the orphans who had been appren-
ticed were treated kindly and educated properly.[32] When
the monthly courts were first established, their jurisdiction in
civil cases was limited to suits involving amounts of not
more than one hundred pounds of tobacco. But in a few
years, the limit was raised, first to five and then to ten
pounds sterling, and later, to sixteen pounds sterling, or sixteen hundred pounds of tobacco.[33] By the end of the cen-

---

[28] York Records, 1633-1694, 2, 3, 8, 14, 67. Lower Norfolk County
Records, 1637-1643, 63, 66, 68, 74, 78.
[29] Essex County Records, 1683-1686, 3, 10, 18, 33. Hening, I, 409.
[30] Accomac Records, 1640-1645, 168, 173, 200, 262. York Records,
1671-1694, 88, 125, 220, 221. Rappahannock Records, 1686-1692, 111,
114, 158. Beverley, History of Va., Book IV, p. 25. Winder MSS.,
I, 204. Mercer, Va. Laws, 64.
[31] Richmond County Records, 1692-1694, 14, 35, 86. Henrico
County Records, 1710-1714, 74, 81, 252; ibid., 1737-1746, 84, 95, 140,
200. Charles City County Records, 1758-1762, 22, 201, 315. Hening, III, 509; V, 490.
[32] York County Records, 1633-1694, 67. Winder MSS., I, 204.
Beverley, History of Va., Book IV, p. 25.
[33] Hening, I, 125, 168, 186, 224, 272, 346, 398. Accomac Records,
1640-1645, 148. Lower Norfolk County Records, 1637-1643, 159-160.
The court of Northampton, a county east of Chesapeake Bay,
could determine finally all causes involving amounts less than
twenty pounds sterling, or 3200 pounds of tobacco. This exception

tury all these restrictions had been removed; and from that time on all civil causes except those of less value than twenty shillings could be determined by the county courts.[84]

But while the jurisdiction of the county courts was thus being broadened at the top, it was being narrowed at the bottom. It was found expedient to relieve them of many petty cases by allowing the commissioners to perform certain judicial acts out of court. So in 1643 it was provided by law that no suit for a debt under the amount of twenty shillings (afterwards twenty-five) should thereafter be heard in the county courts, but that every controversy of this kind should be decided by the magistrate living nearest the creditor. The magistrate was also authorized to commit to prison the litigant who would not comply with his award.[85] From this time until the end of the colonial period, causes involving amounts of not more than twenty-five shillings, or two hundred pounds of tobacco, were determinable by single justices.[86] The judicial authority of single justices was not confined to civil cases, but violations of certain penal laws could also be punished by them.[87] They were to hear complaints of ill-treatment made by servants against their masters, and if they considered the charges well-founded, were to summon the offending masters before the county court. Complaints of servants could also be made directly to the county courts by petition " without the formal process of an action." Furthermore, masters were not allowed to whip Christian white servants naked without an order from a jus-

---

was made against this county because of its distance from James City and the difficulty with which appeals from its court could be prosecuted in the General Court. Hening, I, 346.

[84] Hening, III, 507-508; V, 491. Warwick Records, 1748-1762, 272. Blair, Hartwell, and Chilton, 43, 44. Webb, Virginia Justice, 107.

[85] Hening, I, 273. Hartwell, Blair, and Chilton, 43.

[86] Hening, V, 491. Hartwell, Blair, and Chilton, 43. Winder MSS., I, 204. Webb, Virginia Justice, 203. Mercer, Virginia Laws, 64.

For a few years, single justices could hear causes of the value of 350 pounds of tobacco. Hening, I, 435.

[87] Webb, Virginia Justice, 204.

tice.[38] By these provisions, servants were given easy access to the local judiciary, and the protection of the law was placed in easy reach of them. Appeals from the decisions of single justices were in certain causes allowed to the county courts, but the decisions of the county courts on such appeals were always final.[39] The authority of two justices acting together, one being of the quorum, was greater than that of single magistrates. Proclamations against outlying slaves and warrants for their arrest could be issued by them. They could suppress ordinaries during the intervals between court sessions if the keepers allowed unlawful gaming and drinking on the Sabbath day. By a statute of 1676 (re-enacted next year) any two justices of the quorum were given power to sign probates of wills, and letters of administration.[40]

At first, the criminal jurisdiction of the county courts was limited to petty causes, but it seems that later it was increased so as to include important criminal offenses. This enlargement of the jurisdiction of the local courts was made for the convenience of the people, but the local tribunals were unequal to the new responsibility. So in 1655, by an act of the legislature, this power was taken from them; and it was ordered that offenses " touching life or member " should thereafter be referred to the Quarter Court of the assembly, whichever of them should first be in session. The assembly realized that, in thus restricting the powers of the lower courts, it was departing from English precedent, and was, to that extent, causing their divergence from the line of development which had been followed by the county court system of the mother country. The reason given by the assembly for thus restricting the jurisdiction of the lower courts was that the juries generally empaneled in the sparsely settled counties of Virginia were less informed and

---

[38] Hening, I, 255, 440; III, 448, 449; VI, 357, 358. Calendar Virginia State Papers, I, 99.

[39] Starke, Virginia Justice, 10.

[40] Hening, I, 435; II, 359, 391; III, 86, 397-398. Henrico County Records, 1677-1692, 16-17, 300-301.

less experienced in judicial matters than those in the English shires, and could not, therefore, with equal safety, be entrusted with the fate of criminals charged with high crimes. Thus the law-makers of Virginia realized in this case, as well as in many others, that a constitution which had been made for an old and highly developed society, could not be fitted to a new and rapidly growing state without some adaptation.[41] From this time until the Revolution, no offenses punishable by loss of life or member, unless they were committed by slaves, were cognizable in the county courts.[42] But the county courts could order the ears of slaves to be cut off as a punishment for hog-stealing,[43] and during the last century of the colonial period, the justices could try slaves charged with capital crimes.[44]

In the county courts, as well as in the General Court, decisions were reached by a majority vote of the judges present.[45] Petit juries were called on to decide matters of fact, and offenses were brought before the court by means of presentments and indictments made by the churchwardens and the grand jury.

The offenses which the churchwardens were required to present to the county courts were fornication, adultery, drunkenness, " abusive and blasphemous speaking, absence from church, Sabbath-breaking," and other like violations of the moral code.[46] But the duty of publicly accusing their

---

[41] Hening, I, 397, 398, 476.

[42] Hening, III, 508; V, 491. Webb, Virginia Justice, 107.

[43] But this inhuman punishment was inflicted only for the second offense. Other persons, as well as slaves, were severely punished for hog-stealing. For a good many years, the laws provided that all persons found guilty of hog-stealing for the second time were to be required by the county courts to stand in the pillory two hours with their ears nailed to it, and at the end of that time to have their ears cut loose from the nails. Hening, II, 441; III, 179, 276, 277. Beverley, History of Virginia, Book IV, p. 25.

[44] See pp. 99-101.

[45] Hening, I, 125.

[46] Hening, I, 126, 156, 227. Accomac Records, 1632-1640, 123. Lower Norfolk County Records, 1637-1643, 85, 217, 220, 226.

In every parish, which was a subdivision of a county, there were two churchwardens and a vestry composed of twelve men. Usually

neighbors of disgraceful deeds must have been a hard one to
perform, and so the thankless task was often shirked by
them.[47] The churchwardens had power by law to make
presentments during the entire colonial period, but in the
latter part of it they seem not to have exercised this authority
often.[48]

In 1645, the grand jury found its way into the county
court, where it joined with the churchwardens in acting the
rôle of public accuser. By a statute of this year, it was
provided that grand juries should be empaneled at the mid-

---

there were from two to four parishes in a county, though in some
of the counties there was only one. The parish was not always
bound by the limits of the county, but some of the parishes extended into two counties. The office of churchwarden seems to
have been older in Virginia than that of vestryman, for we find mention of churchwardens as early as 1619, and we know that churchwardens were chosen in Accomac County before the vestry was
appointed.

Vestrymen were elected differently at different times. The first
vestry that is mentioned in the county court records was appointed
by the commissioners of the monthly court, and as late as 1692, an
old vestry was dissolved and a new one chosen by a county court.
Vestrymen were also often elected, especially in the early years, by
a majority of the householders of the parish. But in time there
grew up the custom of allowing the vestries to fill their own vacancies, and so they became self-perpetuating bodies like the county
courts. Every year the vestrymen elected two of their number to
the office of churchwarden.

To the vestrymen and the churchwardens was entrusted the management of the affairs of the parish. They appointed ministers, kept
the churches in repair, bound out orphan children, and laid the
parish levy. Another important duty performed by the vestry was
that of "processioning" lands. Every four years (at one time
every year) they had to go around the lands of every person in the
parish and mark out the bounds and renew the landmarks. This
was a wise provision; for it must have prevented many disputes
over boundaries which would otherwise have arisen, and thus have
removed a very fruitful source of litigation. Hening I, 290, 291;
II, 25, 44, 45; III, 325, 530. Henrico Parish Vestry Book, 1730-
1773, 8, 12, 16, 20-26, 34, 35. Bristol Parish Vestry Book, 1720-
1789, 3, 5, 7, 15, 18, 26. Colonial Records of Virginia, 27, 103, 104.
Jefferson's Notes on Virginia, 116. Richmond County Records,
1692-1694, 56. Accomac Records, 1632-1640, 10, 39. Winder MSS.,
II, 163. Webb, Virginia Justice, 71. Robinson MSS., 235. Beverley, History of Virginia, Book IV, p. 28. Hugh Jones, Present
State of Virginia, 63, 66. Warwick Records, 1748-1762, 78, 81, 342.

[47] Hening, I, 291, 310.

[48] Webb, Virginia Justice, 71. Mercer, Virginia Laws, 286. Beverley, Book IV, p. 28.

summer and March terms of the county courts " to receive all presentments and informations, and to enquire of the breach of all penal laws and other crimes and misdemeanors not touching life or member, to present the same to the court." In 1658, a law was passed providing that grand juries should be empaneled at every court. But the grand jury system did not prove as efficient in the detection of offenses as its advocates hoped it would, and the law was repealed the same year.[49]

But the repeal of this statute proved to be an unwise measure for it left the counties without adequate provision for the detection of offenses. In a year or so it was noticed that the laws were not being properly respected, and a renewal of the grand jury system in the counties was voted by the assembly. By an act of 1662, it was ordered that grand juries should thereafter be empaneled in all the counties, and that all breaches of the penal laws committed within their respective counties should be presented by them to the county courts at the April and December terms.[50] In fifteen years this statute had almost become a dead letter because it had not provided any penalty for non-compliance with its provisions. For this reason, a law was passed in 1677 which provided for a fine of two thousand pounds of tobacco to be imposed on every court that should fail to swear a grand jury once a year, and a fine of two hundred pounds of tobacco on every juror who should be absent from court without a lawful excuse.[51]

From this time until the end of the colonial period, the grand jury was a permanent part of the county court system. By the end of the seventeenth century, it had reached its complete development, and no material changes were made in it from that time until the Revolution. It was the custom during the eighteenth century for the sheriff to summon

[49] Hening, I, 304, 463, 521.
[50] Ibid., II, 74.
[51] Ibid., II, 407, 408.

twenty-four [52] freeholders to be present at the May and November courts. Those that obeyed the summons constituted the grand jury, provided the number that attended was not less than fifteen. If enough jurors were absent to bring the number below fifteen, no jury was empaneled and the absentees were fined.[53]

By 1642 the practice of calling on petit juries to try causes had been introduced in the county courts.[54] A law was passed in that year which gave either party to a controversy pending in any court in the colony the right of having a jury summoned to sit in judgment on his case, provided it was important enough to be tried by a jury.[55] Litigants were not slow to avail themselves of this privilege, and almost immediately we meet with jury trials in the county courts.[56]

From this time on, the county courts referred important causes to juries for trial. The usual practice in the eighteenth century was for a jury of twelve men to be selected from the bystanders every day the court was in session, which was called on to decide all causes that should be tried by a jury.[57] According to the laws that were in force during this century, none but those who possessed property of the value of fifty pounds sterling could serve on juries in the county courts.[58] In the county court, as well as in the Gen-

---

[52] In the latter part of the seventeenth century, the number summoned was twelve. Each juror made an individual report of the offenses that had come within his knowledge. York Records, 1671-1694, 125. Henrico Records, 1677-1692, 32, 33. Elizabeth City County Records, 1684-1699, 4, 93.

[53] Richmond County Records, 1692-1694, 136, 137. Henrico Records, 1710-1714, 55, 110, 193, 273; ibid., 1737-1746, 5, 34, 39. Warwick Records, 1748-1762, 103, 184, 355. Charles City County Records, 1758-1762, 75, 115. Hening, III, 367-368; IV, 232.

[54] Juries are mentioned in the county court records before this time; but they were not empaneled to try causes but only to appraise estates and goods about which suits were pending in the courts. Accomac Records, 1632-1640, 17, 59.

[55] Hening, I, 273.

[56] Accomac Records, 1640-1645, 179, 188, 190, 204, 222.

[57] Hening, I, 474; II, 74; III, 369; V, 525. Essex County Records, 1683-1686, 1, 8, 32, 40, 60. Henrico Records, 1677-1692, 191. Rappahannock Records, 1686-1692, 214. Richmond County Records, 1692-1694, 91.

[58] Hening, III, 176, 370; V, 526.

eral Court, it was the practice in the early years for juries to be kept from food until after they had rendered their verdict.[59] A few instances are recorded in which juries of women were called on to decide questions of fact in cases in which women were charged with witchcraft or of concealing bastard children.[60]

---

[59] Hening, I, 303; II, 74.

[60] Rappahannock Records, 1686-1692, 163. William and Mary College, Quarterly, Jan., 1893, pp. 126-128.

It is not to be inferred from this mention of witchcraft cases that such trials were frequent occurrences, for only a few cases have been found in which persons were charged with this crime. The most noted witchcraft trial in Virginia history was that of Grace Sherwood. On the 7th of December, 1705, Grace Sherwood brought suit in the court of Princess Anne County against Luke Hill and his wife in action of trespass of assault and battery and recovered damages to the amount of twenty shillings. Soon after this, Luke Hill and his wife brought before the same court an accusation of witchcraft against Grace Sherwood. The court in February, 1706, ordered the sheriff to issue an attachment against the body of Grace Sherwood and to summon a jury of matrons for her trial. On the 7th of March the case came up for a hearing, and the jury of twelve women brought in the following verdict: "Wee of ye Jury have Serch[th] Grace Sherwood & have found Two things like titts with several Spotts." This report of the jury left the court in doubt as to what should be done, and Luke Hill sent in a petition to the council asking that Grace Sherwood be prosecuted before the General Court. This petition was referred to the attorney-general for his opinion, who said that the charge was too general to warrant a prosecution before the General Court. He also said that the case should be examined again by the court of Princess Anne, and if sufficient grounds were found for a trial by the General Court, the accused should be sent to the public jail at Williamsburg. He would then prosecute her before the General Court if an indictment against her were made by the grand jury. The case was again taken up in the Princess Anne court, and a jury of matrons was again summoned. But the court had some difficulty in getting a jury to serve, and the trial was delayed for a while. Finally on the 5th of July the court, with the consent of the accused, decided to appeal to the ordeal of water to determine her guilt or innocence. The sheriff was ordered to take her on the 10th of July out and duck her in deep water, but was to be very careful not to endanger her life. She swam when she was thrown into the water, and after she was brought out, a jury of women again examined her. The verdict brought in by these women was about the same as the one reported by the jury on the 7th of March. The sheriff was then ordered to kep her in jail until she could be tried again; but it is probable that all proceedings against her were dropped, as further mention of the case is not found in the records. William and Mary College Quarterly, IV, 18-20. Lower Norfolk County Antiquary, IV, 139-141; III, 34-38.

The justices of the county courts, like the judges of the General Court, were not always closely bound by laws in giving their decisions. The early commissioners sometimes invented penalties and fitted them to offenses without the guidance of any legal precedent. The unique way in which this was done argued more for the originality of the judges than for their knowledge of the law.[61]

There was no lack of variety in the punishments that the early justices inflicted on criminals. Fines were imposed, and often resort was had to the lash to induce offenders to repent of their misdeeds. As a rule, the number of stripes given did not exceed thirty-nine, but they were generally made on the bare back.[62] In the early records of Lower Norfolk County, three cases appear in which culprits were punished by receiving one hundred lashes on the bare shoulders.[63] One case is also given in the records of Essex County in which this punishment took a very severe form. The court, on a certain occasion, ordered the sheriff to give an offender one hundred and twenty lashes on the bare back.[64] However, law-breakers were seldom subjected to such harsh treatment, and it seems that, on the whole, the penal laws of Virginia as interpreted by the judiciary in the

---

[61] See pp. 90-91. The following example of the originality of the justices in devising penalties is given in the Accomac Records, under date of September 8, 1634. A woman for calling another a prostitute was ordered to be drawn across a creek at the stern of a boat, unless she acknowledged her fault in church the next Sunday between the first and second lesson. Accomac County Records, 1632-1640, 20.

[62] In the records of York County, two instances are recorded in which offenders were ordered to be whipped until the blood came. York Records, 1671-1694, 138, 221. Accomac Records, 1632-1640, 20, 37, 47; ibid., 1640-1645, 49, 88, 200.

[63] In one of these cases the offense was a mutiny of slaves against an overseer in the absence of their master. In one of the other two cases, a woman had wrongfully charged a man with being the father of a bastard child born of his servant. In the other, a woman-servant had falsely accused her mistress of acts of unchastity. Lower Norfolk County Records, 1637-1643, 12, 14, 15, 16.

[64] Essex County Records, 1683-1686, 49.

These are the only examples of such undue severity that have been found though it is not claimed that no others are on record.

colonial period were not harsher than could be expected at
that time.

The early commissioners did not rely solely on physical
punishments for the correction of wrong-doing, but some of
the penalties that they ordered must have appealed strongly
to the self-esteem of those who had brought themselves under
the censure of the court. Slanderers frequently were required to ask pardon of the injured parties in church or in
open court, and were sometimes compelled to sit in the
stocks on Sunday during divine service. Those who had
abused their neighbors might also be subjected to the humilia-
tion of lying neck and heels together at the church door.[65]
Fornication and adultery were very much frowned upon by
the county courts. In the early years, men and women who
had committed these sins were sometimes whipped, and
sometimes were compelled to acknowledge their fault in
church before the whole congregation. A few instances are
recorded in which women who had erred from the path of
virtue or had slandered their neighbors were compelled to
make public confession while standing on stools in the
church, with white sheets wrapped around them and white
wands in their hands.[66] Transgressors did not always go
through this terrible ordeal without demurring. In Lower
Norfolk County we find a woman refusing to do penance
properly, and even going so far as to cut her sheet. But the
court would brook no disobedience to its orders, and obstinacy on the part of the criminal only increased the severity of
the original sentence. In the same county a woman was sentenced by the court to ask forgiveness in church for having
slandered one of her neighbors. Having refused to comply
with this order, she was summoned before the court to
answer for her contempt. She did not obey this summons,
and the commissioners, in her absence, voted an order which

---

[65] Accomac Records, 1632-1640, 59, 112, 145, 151; ibid., 1640-1645,
49, 88, 200.

[66] Accomac Records, 1632-1640, 123, 145. Lower Norfolk County
Records, 1637-1643, 219, 226. Accomac Records, 1640-1645, 200.

showed that they were not in a mood to tolerate further
obstinacy on her part. The decree was as follows: " The
sheriff shall take her to the house of a commissioner and
there she shall receive twenty lashes; she is then to be taken
to church the next Sabbath to make confession according to
the former order of the court. If she refuses, she is to be
taken to a commissioner and to be given thirty lashes, and
again given opportunity to do penance in church. If she
still refuses to obey the order of court, she is then to receive
fifty lashes. If she continues in her contempt, she is to
receive fifty lashes, and thereafter fifty every Monday until
she performs her penance." [67]

The oldest county court proceedings that are now extant
are those of Accomac, which date from 1632. These records are particularly interesting because of the unique
methods employed by the commissioners in their administration of justice in the first half of the seventeenth century.
These early commissioners seemed often to consult the dictates of expediency in rendering their decisions, and frequently prescribed such punishments as would wring from
crime an income to the community. Indeed, from the
penalties that they attached to certain offenses, one would
think that the judges inclined to the belief that the wicked-
ness of man should be harnessed and made to do service in
the cause of righteousness. A few cases are recorded in
which wrong-doers were required to build a pair of stocks
and dedicate them to the county by sitting in them during
divine worship, and in 1638 a man who had been guilty of
the sin of fornication was ordered to build a ferry-boat for
the use of the people. [68] We also find a court in 1634 ordering
a man, for abusing another, to " daub the church as soon as
the roof can be repaired." [69] On another occasion, disobedience to a country regulation regarding the carrying of

[67] Lower Norfolk County Records, 1637-1643, 121, 137.
[68] Accomac Records, 1632-1640, 28, 69, 123. Lower Norfolk County Records, 1637-1643, 13.
[69] Accomac Records, 1632-1640, 16.

arms was punished by requiring the offenders to repair to the church the following Saturday and pull up all the weeds growing in the churchyard and the paths leading to it.[70]

Some of these unusual modes of punishment, ducking and pillorying for example, were employed by the courts in the later, as well as in the earlier, part of the colonial period. By laws passed late in the eighteenth century, it was provided that ducking-stools, stocks and pillories should be erected in every county.

For the punishment of breaches of the penal laws committed by servants, a special arrangement had to be made, as they could not pay the fines imposed on them by the court. Additions of time to their terms of service were sometimes made, and in the eighteenth century, it was the custom for the court to allow servants to bind themselves out to a term of service to any one who would pay their fines. But if they could not get any one to assume their fines, they had to undergo corporal punishment and receive twenty-five stripes for every 500 pounds of tobacco of the fine.[71]

The justices had many duties to perform in addition to those of trying causes. They ordered the opening of new roads and saw that surveyors appointed by them kept the highways open and cleared.[72] The levy of the county was apportioned by them, and the lists of tithables were sometimes taken either by themselves or by officers chosen by them for that purpose.[73] The justices also licensed taverns

[70] Accomac Records, 1640-1645, 88.

[71] Hening, III, 267, 268; V, 507, 508. Webb, Virginia Justice, 106, 291. Essex Records, 1683-1686, 5; ibid., 1695-1699, 59. Virginia Gazette, August 19, 1737. Robinson MSS., 53. Rappahannock County Records, 1686-1692, 55, 147.

[72] Hening, II, 103; VI, 65. Essex County Records, 1683-1686, 97. Rappahannock Records, 1686-1692, 16, 46, 163, 212. Henrico Records, 1737-1746, 64, 147, 168, 231.

[73] Hening, II, 357. Henrico Records, 1677-1692, 186, 288, 403. Essex Records, 1695-1699, 40, 86, 87. Elizabeth City County Records, 1684-1699, 98, 172. Beverley, History of Virginia, Book IV, pp. 19-20. According to one of Bacon's Laws, representatives of the people were to assist the justices in laying the county levy.

and regulated the prices at which drinks could be sold.[14]
Another important duty of the court was to issue certificates for land grants. Every "adventurer" who brought
over emigrants to Virginia was entitled to fifty acres of
land for every person transported. These grants were made
by the governor upon certificates given by the county courts
stating the number of persons the claimant had landed.[15]

The county courts were also required to hear complaints
and to examine claims. Once before every session of the
assembly, a court was held for these purposes, public notice
of it having been given beforehand. All claims for dues
from the general government were examined, and the just
ones were certified to and sent on to the assembly with the
recommendation that they be allowed. If the people had
any grievances against the government, they were at liberty
to bring them before this court to be likewise sent on to the
assembly.[16] During a considerable part of the seventeenth
century, the county courts had the power to make or to
assist in making the by-laws of their respective counties.[17]

We see, therefore, that in the county government there
were no well-defined limits separating the judiciary from the

---

[14] Hening, II, 19; III, 396, 397; VI, 71-73. Elizabeth City County
Records, 1684-1699, 236. Henrico Records, 1737-1746, 25, 68, 102,
133, 210, 308. Webb, Virginia Justice, 108.

[15] Accomac Records, 1640-1645, 43, 96. Lower Norfolk County
Records, 1637-1643, 5, 80, 125. Henrico Records, 1710-1714, 2, 12.
Rappahannock Records, 1686-1692, 5, 60, 85, 151.

[16] Hening, II, 405, 421; III, 43, 44; VII, 528; VIII, 316. Essex
Records, 1683-1686, 14, 15, 18. Hartwell, Blair, and Chilton, 39.

[17] This power began to be exercised at an early date, and in 1662,
it was recognized by law. Some years later representatives of the
people met with the justices and took part in making the by-laws for
the counties. By an order of the Committee of Trade and Plantations given in 1683 all laws empowering the county courts to make
by-laws were to be repealed; but the governor was instructed to
allow the assembly to pass a law providing that by-laws be made
by the counties or parishes with the consent of the governor and
council. Whether such a law was passed does not appear, but it
is certain that in a few years (1691), the county courts had been
deprived of the power to make by-laws for the counties. Accomac
Records, 1640-1645, 88, 89. William and Mary College Quarterly,
II, 58, 59. Hening, II, 35, 171, 172, 357, 441. Virginia Magazine of
History and Biography, VIII, 186. Sainsbury MSS., 1682-1686, 51.

legislature and the executive. Nor were the lines that divided the county courts from the other branches of the colonial government sharply drawn. The Burgesses chosen by the counties were very often justices of the peace, and so the county courts and the assembly were kept in close relation with each other.[78] During a part of the seventeenth century, the county courts were in like manner connected with the General Court. Councillors were not ineligible to the office of justice of the peace, and by a law of 1624, they were empowered to sit in the court of any county, even if they were not in the commission, and were authorized to hold a court on occasions of emergency in the absence of the quorum.[79] The interdependence thus established between the higher and lower tribunals must have been a great advantage to the latter, for it not only gave the inexperienced justices the benefit of the advice of a councillor, but it also enabled the decisions of the Quarter and county courts to be rendered with something like uniformity. But there was one objection to allowing the councillors this privilege. It permitted the Quarter Court to assist in giving decisions, the responsibility for which had to be borne by the county courts. For this reason a provision was put in one of Bacon's laws, passed in 1676, forbidding councillors to vote with the justices in the county courts.[80]

In the records that have been examined no mention is made of any great abuses in the practice of the county courts, and on the whole, justice seems to have beeen administered fairly by them. And yet there were certain defects in the county court system which were unfavorable to

[78] Lower Norfolk County Records, 1637-1643, 16, 17, 36, 189. Accomac Records, 1640-1645, 115, 118, 217, 343. Henrico Records, 1677-1692, 133, 228, 244, 403; ibid., 1710-1714, 39, 115, 202, 266; ibid., 1737-1746, 128. Elizabeth City County Records, 1684-1699, 12, 244. Essex Records, 1695-1699, 33, 40, 86, 87.

In 1714, seventy per cent of the Burgesses were justices. Virginia Magazine of History and Biography, II, 3-15.

[79] Hening, I, 224. Lower Norfolk County Records, 1637-1643, 160. Accomac Records, 1640-1645, 149.

[80] Hening, II, 358.

good government in the counties. As the people had no voice, either direct or indirect, in the selection of justices, public opinion was probably not as effective in restraining the judges from unfair decisions as it should have been. Besides, the custom of filling vacancies in the court on the nomination of the justices made the court a self-perpetuating body. The justices would naturally be inclined to give the vacant places on the bench to their friends and relatives, and so it was easy for a few families to get and keep a monopoly of the government in each county.

But despite these defects, the county court system was well adapted to the conditions that obtained in Virginia in colonial times. From the experience gained from the performance of their judicial and administrative duties, the justices learnt much of the art of government, and were thus qualified for taking part in the organization of the commonwealth government when Virginia severed her relations with Great Britain. The fact that Virginia had a numerous class of men who had already known the responsibilities of governing, no doubt, accounts, in large measure, for the absence of radicalism in the constitutional changes made in 1776. To the opportunities for political training afforded by the county courts and the other governmental agencies of the colony, Virginia was also largely indebted for the number and prominence of her leaders in the struggles for independence.

The county courts were not only a training-school for statesmen, but were also incidentally an agency for the education of the people. "Court-day was a holiday for all the country-side, especially in the fall and spring. From all directions came in the people on horseback, in wagons, and afoot. On the court-house green assembled, in indiscriminate confusion, people of all classes, the hunter from the backwoods, the owner of a few acres, the grand proprietor, and the grinning, needless negro. Old debts were settled, and new ones made; there were auctions, transfers of property, and, if election times were near, stump-speaking." [81] These public gatherings brought the people in contact with each other, and gave the ignorant an opportunity to learn from the more enlightened. The education that comes from association with people is a kind that is particularly needed in a society in which the inhabitants are isolated from each other; and, therefore, the educational advantages afforded by the monthly meetings at the county seats atoned to some extent for the lack of adequate opportunities for school education in colonial Virginia.

Circuit Courts.—As the General Court was held only at the capital, appeals from the counties could not be prosecuted in it without considerable delay and inconvenience. So there arose the need for an appellate court to act as intermediary between the higher and lower tribunals. The assembly realized this, and soon after the Restoration, attempted to remedy this defect in the Virginia judiciary by the formation of a new court. In 1662 a law was passed providing for the establishment of circuit courts, which were to be held once a year in every county. The colony was divided into circuits, and to each was assigned the governor and one councillor or two councillors. During the month of August, these judges of the General Court were to hold courts in every county of their respective circuits on the days regularly appointed for the county courts.

Whenever a circuit court was held in a county, all appeals that had been allowed since the preceding March by the regular courts of that county were to be brought before it for trial. Appeals from the county courts that were allowed from October to December were to be tried by the General Court. The reason why appeals were to be taken to the General Court during these months and not during the spring and summer, was that the sessions of the General Court were held oftener in winter than in summer. The decisions of the circuit court were not final but could be appealed from to the assembly or the General Court. When-

---

[81] Ingle, Virginia Local Institutions, J. H. U. Studies, III, 90. Hugh Jones, Present State of Virginia, 49.

ever the judges of a circuit court were the governor and one
councillor, appeals from it were to be allowed to the assembly; but when the itinerant judges were two councillors, appeals from their decisions were to be tried by the General
Court.[82]   But this new tribunal was short-lived, for the law
which brought it into being was repealed in December of this
same year.   The circuit courts were discontinued because of
the great expense incurred in holding them.[83]

Courts of Examination.—In the early years, before the
special courts of examination had grown up, all persons who were charged with any violations of the
penal laws, except those who were punished by loss of
life or member, were brought before the county courts
for examination.   These causes were determined by the
county courts, except those which the justices saw fit to
refer to the governor and council, which were sent on to
the Quarter Court for trial.[84]   It seems, however, that important criminal offenses in the early years were not given a
preliminary hearing in the county courts before they were
brought before the Quarter Court for trial.   But before the
end of the seventeenth century there had grown up a well-
defined system for the examination of prisoners in the
counties.[85]   Whenever a justice issued a warrant for the
arrest of a criminal charged with an offense which, in his
opinion, was not cognizable in the county court, he ordered
the sheriff to summon his fellow magistrates together in a
special court of examination, which was held within ten days
after the issuance of the warrant.   The offender and his
witnesses were brought before this court and examined, and
if he was found innocent of the charge brought against him
he was discharged.   If, however, the evidence gave grounds

[82] Hening, II, 64, 65.
[83] Ibid., II, 179.
[84] Ibid., I, 304.   Accomac Records, 1632-1640, 43, 47; ibid., 1640-
1645, 270.
[85] We do not find a law recognizing the existence of courts of
examination until 1704, but we know that such a court had been
established in Rappahannock County as early as 1690.   Rappahannock Records, 1686-1692, 163.   Hening, III, 225.

for a trial the case was sent to the next grand jury court of the county, provided it was matter of which the county court took cognizance. But if it proved to be a case over which the county court had no jurisdiction, it was sent up to the General Court for determination. Whenever a cause was referred to the General Court, the prisoner was turned over to the custody of the sheriff to be taken at once to the public jail at the capital, unless the offense was a bailable one, in which case he was given twenty days in which to find bail.[86] This method of examining criminals was employed from the last decade of the seventeenth century to the end of the colonial period. By means of these special courts criminal cases were all sifted, and only those in which there was some chance of conviction were passed on to the General Court. In this way criminal offenses were disposed of with less expense than they would have been if all of them had been tried directly by the General Court.

Slave Courts.—A good deal of special legislation for the punishment of slaves is found in the colonial laws. When a runaway slave was caught, he was taken from one constable to another until he was brought back to his owner. Each constable who took part in conveying the fugitive back to his master whipped him before turning him over to the next constable. If it was not known to whom the fugitive belonged, he was confined in the county jail and a notice of his capture was posted on the court-house door. At the end of two months, if he was not claimed by his owner, he was sent to the public jail at Williamsburg and was kept in the custody of the sheriff there until his master was found. In the Virginia Gazette were published notices of all such fugitives, in which minute descriptions of their personal appearance were given.[87] Two justices, one being of the quorum,

---

[86] Hening, III, 389-391; V, 541, 542. Webb, Virginia Justice, 109-115. Starke, Virginia Justice, 114-120. Henrico Records, 1719-1724, 137, 138; ibid., 1737-1746, 87, 166, 252, 253.

[87] Hening, III, 456-457; IV, 168-169; V, 552-554; VI, 363-365. Virginia Gazette, June 3, 1737; July 7 and September 29, 1768; December 7, 1769.

could issue proclamations against outlying slaves, ordering
them to return to their masters. These orders were to be
read every Sunday twice in succession in every church in
the county immediately after divine service. After this
announcement had once been made any outlying slave who
failed to obey it could be killed by any one without fear of
punishment.[88] Besides, the county courts for some years
had the power to punish incorrigible and runaway slaves
by castration. But by 1769 the assembly had come to realize
that this penalty was " revolting to the principles' of human-
ity " and was " often disproportionate to the offense." By
a law passed in this year, the county courts were deprived of
the power to order the castration of outlying slaves and were
limited in the use of this punishment to attempts at rape
made by negroes against white women.[89] As has already
been shown,[90] there was no law extending the benefit of
clergy to slaves until 1732, and even after that time, this
privilege was not allowed in all cases in which it could be
claimed by freemen. There was also some discrimination
against slaves in the punishments prescribed by the laws for
penal offenses.[91]

The testimony of Indians, negroes, and mulattoes, bond
and free, was allowed in the trial of slaves for capital crimes.
For a while persons of that description who professed
Christianity and " could give some account of the principles
of the Christian religion," served as witnesses in the cases
regularly tried by the General Court. But their testimony
was very unreliable and was rejected by some juries while it
was admitted by others. Just decisions could not be reached
so long as they were based on such untrustworthy evidence,
and so in 1732 it was enacted by the assembly that no negro,
Indian, or mulatto, bond or free, should thereafter be al-

---

[88] Hening, III, 460; VI, 110.
[89] Hening, III, 460, 461; IV, 132; VIII, 358.
[90] See page 69.
[91] Ballagh, History of Slavery in Virginia, 85-88. Hening, VI,
106.

lowed to bear witness in court except in the trial of slaves charged with capital offenses. After this kind of testimony was excluded, it frequently happened the persons so discriminated against were relieved from paying their just debts because they could not be proved in court. Therefore, it became necessary to modify the rule against negro and Indian testimony, and in 1744 it was provided by law that free Christian negroes, Indians, and mulattoes should be allowed to bear witness for or against any negro, Indian, or mulatto, free or slave, in any court in the colony in both civil and criminal cases.[92]

Prior to 1692, there were no special courts for the trial of slaves charged with capital crimes. Like freemen who were accused of the same offenses, they were never sentenced to death except at Jamestown and only after they had been given a trial by jury. Not only was this method of trial expensive, but it also prevented a speedy administration of justice. But the punishment of negroes for capital offenses had to be inflicted without delay if it was to be most effective in deterring other slaves from crime. For these reasons a special court of oyer and terminer for the trial of slaves was created in 1692 by an act of assembly. This law provided that the sheriff of a county should notify the governor whenever he had arrested a slave for a capital crime. Upon receipt of this notice, the governor was to issue a special commission of oyer and terminer to such persons of the county as he should deem fit, and the persons so named— who were, as a rule, justices of the peace—were to meet at once in a court at the county seat. The prisoner was to be brought before this court and tried without the aid of a jury.

Other laws were passed from time to time which reaffirmed and enlarged the provisions of this act. By a statute of 1705 masters were to be allowed to appear in defense of their slaves " as to matters of fact, but not as to

---

[92] Hening, IV, 127, 327; V, 244, 24⁵: VI, 106. Henrico County Records, 1737-1746, 254, 285.

technicalities of procedure," and were to be indemnified for the loss of their slaves whenever they were executed by order of the court. This indemnity was an inducement to the people to report the crimes of their slaves to the authorities. When the law was revised in 1723, it was provided that the testimony of negroes, Indians, or mulattoes, bond or free, when supported by " pregnant circumstances or the testimony of one or more credible witnesses," should be accepted by the court as sufficient evidence for conviction or acquittal. If a non-Christian negro, Indian, or mulatto should give false testimony he was to be severely punished. His ears were to be nailed to the pillory one hour each and were to be cut loose from the nails, after which he was to receive thirty-nine lashes " on his bare back, well-laid on." In 1748, unanimity of the judges present was required for conviction ; but by a law of 1772, sentences could be voted by any four of the justices, being a majority of those present.

But even this method of trying slaves was attended with some inconvenience, for the commissions of oyer and terminer given by the governor for every court could not be sent to the counties without considerable trouble and expense. Besides, the time limit of these commissions was sometimes reached before sentences had been given by the courts. These objections were met by a law passed in 1765, which provided that the justices should be given a standing commission of oyer and terminer empowering them to try all criminal offenses committed by slaves in their respective counties. Whenever a warrant was issued for the arrest of a slave charged with a capital crime, the justices of the county were summoned by the sheriff to meet at once in a special court. Any four or more of the justices who obeyed this summons were to constitute a court, before which the prisoner was arraigned for trial. Sentences were given as before without the assistance of a jury.

Clergy was allowed by the slave courts for those offenses to which it had been extended by law. For crimes without the benefit of clergy, hanging was the usual punishment,[93] though occasionally the death penalty came in a more barbarous form. One instance has been found in which a slave was burnt for murder,[94] and another is given in which the heads and quarters of some negroes who had been hanged were set up in the county as a warning to their fellow-slaves.[95] The sentences given by the court were executed without delay. In Henrico county in the early part of the eighteenth century slaves convicted by this court seem usually to have been hanged on the first Friday after their trial, and two cases are recorded in which only two days elapsed between the trial of a slave and his execution.[96] By such a speedy administration of justice the criminal was deprived of the opportunity of seeking a pardon from the governor, and, in 1748, it was provided by law that death sentences against slaves should never be executed except in cases of conspiracy, rebellion, or insurrection until after ten days had elapsed.[97]

The prohibition of trials by jury in the slave courts was not an unjust discrimination against the slaves. On the contrary, it was an advantage to the slave that he was tried by the justices and not by a jury, especially during the period when convictions could not be made except by a unanimous vote of the judges present. For the justices were better qualified than an average jury to decide causes, and were less liable to give unjust sentences.[98]

Courts of Hustings.—In 1705, Governor Nott was in-

---

[93] Hening, III, 102, 103, 269-270; IV, 126-128; VI, 104-108; VIII, 137, 138, 522, 523. Calendar Virginia State Papers, I, 194. Henrico Records, 1710-1714, 225, 308; ibid., 1719-1724, 39, 43, 75, 159; ibid., 1737-1746, 254, 284, 415. Warwick Records, 1748-1762, 128, 129, 299, 300. Charles City County Records, 1758-1762, 221, 222, 245. Ballagh, History of Slavery in Virginia, 82, 83. Dinwiddie Papers, I, 384.

[94] Virginia Gazette, February 18, 1737.

[95] Virginia Magazine of History and Biography, I, 329, 330.

[96] Henrico Records, 1719-1724, 39, 159, 547; ibid., 1737-1746, 284-285.

[97] Starke, Virginia Justice, 272. Hening, VI, 106.

[98] Ballagh, History of Slavery in Virginia, 85.

structed by the Queen to recommend to the assembly the
enactment of a law which would bring about the establishment of towns in Virginia. In obedience to this order, the
assembly in 1705 passed a law, which was to take effect
three years later, designating certain places as ports, from
which all exports from the colony were to be sent, and into
which all imports were to be received.[99] It was thought that
the monoply of the colony's foreign commerce thus given to
these shipping points would cause towns to grow up around
them, and by this same act a detailed scheme of government
was mapped out for these towns.[100] The assembly seemed to
think that towns could be legislated into being despite the
fact that economic conditions in Virginia were unfavorable
to city life. To planters who lived on the navigable rivers
with wharfs at their doors, the law requiring them to take
their tobacco miles away to load it at a would-be-town
seemed a useless and oppressive measure.[101] It was not long
before the folly of this act of paternalism had become plainly
apparent to the Lords of Trade, as no attempt was made to
settle these towns.[102] They recommended that the Queen
repeal the law, and in 1710 Governor Spottswood issued a
proclamation declaring it null and void.[103]

While the assembly and the Lords of Trade failed in their
attempt to impose city life on rural Virginia, commerce and
trade did select a few places for towns. The first of the
towns to grow into such importance as to require a court
of Hustings was Williamsburg, the capital. In 1722, Williamsburg received a charter from the King which constituted it a city and gave it a separate government. The management of the affairs of the city was entrusted to a mayor,
recorder, six aldermen and twelve councilmen. The King

---

[99] Other abortive attempts to establish towns were made by the
assembly prior to this time. Hening, I, 362, 397. Ingle, Local
Institutions of Virginia, J. H. U. Studies, III, 101-103.
[100] Hening, III, 404-419.
[101] Byrd MSS., II, 162-165.
[102] Sainsbury MSS., 1706-1714, 215.
[103] Henrico Records, 1710-1714, 17.

appointed the first mayor, recorder, and aldermen, who were to elect twelve councilmen to hold office during good behavior. Every year at the feast of St. Andrew the mayor, aldermen, and councilmen were to meet and select one of the aldermen to be mayor for the ensuing year. Whenever vacancies occurred in the board of aldermen by the death or resignation of any of its members, they were to be filled from the common council by the mayor, recorder, aldermen, and common council. When a vacancy occurred in the common council, the mayor, recorder, aldermen, and common council chose some freeholder to fill it. The government of the town was thus placed in the hands of officers in the election of whom the people had no voice at all.

The mayor, recorder (who was to be learned in the law), and the six aldermen were the judges of the Court of Hustings, and were also justices of the peace in Williamsburg. But no alderman was to sit in the Court of Hustings of Williamsburg, unless he was also commissioned a justice of the peace in some county. The mayor, recorder, and aldermen performed legislative, administrative, and judicial duties; and so in Williamsburg, as well as in the counties, the judiciary was closely connected with the other branches of the local government. The meetings of the Hustings Court were to be held monthly.[104] The court was at first limited in its jurisdiction to those causes in which the amounts involved did not exceed twenty pounds sterling, or 4000 pounds of tobacco, and appeals were allowed to the General Court. The jurisdiction of the court was enlarged from time to time, and in 1736 it was provided by an act of assembly that the court of Hustings of Williamsburg was to " have jurisdiction and hold plea of all actions, personal and mixt, and attachments, whereof any county court within this colony, by law, have or can take cognizance." This court also decided chancery causes, and examined crimi-

---

[104] Charter of Williamsburg, published in the William and Mary College Quarterly, X, 84-91.

nals that were sent from Williamsburg to the General Court and oyer and terminer courts for trial, but it seems not to have had authority to try slaves charged with capital offenses.[105]

In 1736, Norfolk was granted a charter which contained about the same provisions as the one given to Williamsburg in 1722. The governmental machinery provided for by this charter was almost an exact replica of that of Williamsburg, except that in Norfolk the number of aldermen was to be eight instead of six, and the number of councilmen, sixteen instead of twelve. In Norfolk, as in Williamsburg, the mayor, recorder, and aldermen constituted the Court of Hustings, which was at first to take cognizance only of those causes in which the amounts involved did not exceed twenty pounds sterling, or 4000 pounds of tobacco. The jurisdiction of the Norfolk court was extended by subsequent statutes, and during the last years of the colonial period the courts of Norfolk and Williamsburg exercised the same jurisdiction. These were the only cities in which corporation courts were organized before the Revolution.[106]

Coroners' Courts.—Coroners were appointed by the governor, and justices of the peace were usually, though not always, selected for the office. In 1702 the number of coroners in the different counties varied from one to four. These offices had ministerial, as well as judicial duties to perform. When a sheriff was personally interested in a suit or was for any other reason disqualified from serving the county court, the process could be directed to one of the coroners and could be executed by him. But the main duty of the coroners was to hold inquests over the bodies of persons who had met with violent deaths. Whenever

---

[105] Hening, IV, 542; V, 204-207; VIII, 401-402. Webb, Virginia Justice, 105, 108.
[106] Charter of Norfolk, published in Local Institutions of Virginia, appendix, by Ingle, J. H. U. Studies, 3d series. Hening, IV, 541, 542; VI, 261-265; VIII, 153, 154. Virginia Gazette, November 19, 1736

the occasion for an inquest arose a coroner would order the constable of his precinct to summon twenty-four freeholders to the coroner's court. From this number a jury of twelve was chosen to view the body and make a report as to the cause of the death. Witnesses were summoned if necessary, and a few instances are recorded in which resort was had to the ordeal of touch to decide the guilt or innocence of persons accused of murder. In 1656, a jury of inquest was sworn in Northampton County to examine the body of a man supposed to have been murdered. This jury gave the following verdict: " Have reviewed the body of Paul Rynnuse, late of this county dec'd, and have caused Mr. Wm. Custis (the person questioned) to touch the face and stroke of the said Paul Rynuse (which he very willingly did). But no sign did appear unto us of question in law." [107]

Military Courts.—The militia of the colony included all the able-bodied men between the ages of sixteen, eighteen, or twenty, and sixty (these were the different limits at different times), except certain classes of persons who were exempted from militia duty by law. In 1721, the militiamen constituted about one-sixth of the entire white population of the colony. The militia of every county was organized into a regiment, which was commanded by a colonel or an inferior officer. It was necessary for the militia officers to call their men together frequently for the purpose of drilling them. Each captain was to hold what was called a private muster for the members of his company four times a year, or oftener if the commander of the regiment required it. In addition to these private musters, a general muster was held in each county usually once or twice a

---

[107] Webb, Virginia Justice, 97-104, 296. Starke, Virginia Justice, 106-113. Henrico Records, 1677-1692, 146, 191; ibid., 1737-1746, 334. Surry County Records, 1645-1672, 278. Virginia Magazine of History and Biography, I, 364-373. Virginia Magazine of History and Biography, V, 40.
In the trial of Grace Sherwood for witchcraft (see p. 87), the ordeal was appealed to by a county court.

year, at which all the militiamen of the county were to be present.[108]

These musters could not be conducted properly unless the officers were given power to punish their men for insubordination, absence from the drills, and other delinquencies. Accordingly, it was provided that whenever a militiaman should refuse to obey an order of an officer at a muster, the ranking officer present could punish the offender by imposing a fine on him or by ordering him to be bound neck and heels together for a few minutes. If he repeated the offense, he was to be tried by the captains and field-officers present, who by a majority vote could send him to prison for a term not exceeding ten days. At all the musters, general as well as private, the captains were to keep a record of the offenses and delinquencies in attendance and equipment of all the men of their respective companies, and were to report the same to the court martial. The court martial was convened once a year at the county seat on the day following that of the general muster. In this military court sat a majority or all of the captains and field-officers of the county. The court inquired into the ages and capabilities of all those on the muster list, and decided which ones should be dropped on the grounds of old age or physical disability. It also inquired into the absences and other delinquencies reported by the captains and imposed fines for the same.[109]

Apparently there never were any regular parish courts in colonial times, though there is an intimation in the records of Accomac that the vestry of that county in the early years had judicial powers in cases involving certain violations of the moral code.[110] In 1656, a court was established for

---

[108] In 1674 general musters appear to have been held oftener than twice a year. General Court Records, 1670-1676, 197.

[109] Sainsbury MSS., 1720-1730, 30. Winder MSS., I, 206. Hening, II, 246, 247; III, 335-342; IV, 118-124; V, 16-21; VI, 530-536; VII, 93-99, 536-538.

[110] The Accomac County court decreed in one case that "all who have been freemen since 1634 and have not contributed towards the

Bristol, an outlying parish of Henrico and Charles City counties; but the judges of this court were not the vestrymen, but were the commissioners living in the parish. The jurisdiction of the court was the same as that of the county courts, but in all cases appeals were to be allowed to Charles City and Henrico county courts.[111]

When Lord Culpeper and others were granted the territory known as the Northern Neck,[112] which lies between the Rappahannock and Potomac Rivers, they were given power to establish courts-baron and courts-leet and to hold frank-pledge of all the inhabitants. The court-leet was to have jurisdiction over all the tenants and other inhabitants of the hundred in which it was held, except those that had received land grants from the governor and council prior to 1669. The jurisdiction of the court-baron was to be limited to causes involving amounts not exceeding forty shillings in value and appeals were to be allowed to the Quarter Court.[113] However, it is more than probable that this bit of feudalism never, in actual practice, found a place in the Virginia judiciary, for no mention has been found of any attempt to carry out these instructions.

---

charges of the church officers' business shall be liable to stand to the judgment of the vestry." At another time (1641) the vestry ordered a servant to stand in a white sheet in church for the sin of fornication, but this decree was set aside by the court. Accomac Records, 1632-1640, 53; ibid., 1640-1645, 97.

[111] By a special provision a similar court was to be established in 1679 for a frontier settlement to be made by Captain Lawrence Smith and Colonel William Byrd. Hening, I, 424; II, 450-451.

[112] The grant was first made in 1649, and was renewed in 1669.

[113] Sainsbury MSS., 1640-1691, 189-193.

CHAPTER IV.

Court Officials and Lawyers.

By the year 1634, when the shires were organized, the development of the colony had gone far enough to necessitate the appointment of sheriffs for the counties.[1] Before that time, the duties of the sheriffalty were, as we have seen, performed mainly by the provost marshal, though the commander of the hundred also sometimes executed the orders of the governor.[2] As late as 1633, we find the provost marshal making arrests, warning the court, imprisoning offenders, and inflicting on them such punishments as ducking, tying them by the heels, and setting them in the stocks. The fee which he received for the performance of each of these duties was set by the assembly. He was also entrusted with the care of prisoners, and had to provide them with " diet and lodging." For this he received a compensation which was paid by the prisoners themselves, and the amount of which was determined by agreement with them.[3]

It seems that the monthly courts at first elected sheriffs,[4] but soon it became the custom for the governor and council to appoint them on the recommendation of the county commissioners. Vacancies were temporarily filled by the commissioners.[5] According to a later practice, the office devolved on the justices in rotation. The oldest justice in the commission first served a term of one year, and then all

---

[1] Hening, I, 224. Accomac Records, 1632-1640, 17.

[2] Virginia Court Book, 1623-1626, July 12. Robinson MSS., 58. Hening, I, 176, 201, 220. Colonial Records of Virginia, 20. Accomac Records, 1632-1640, 6, 8, 10, 16, 20.

[3] Robinson MSS., 58. Hening, I, 176, 177, 201, 220.

[4] Accomac Records, 1632-1640, 18.

[5] Robinson MSS., 168. Lower Norfolk County Records, 1637-1643, 220. Accomac Records, 1640-1645, 73, 74, 357. Hening, I, 259, 392, 442, 471.

the others followed in succession.[6] However, the old method
of selecting sheriffs was afterwards revived, and from the
end of the seventeenth century to the Revolution, sheriffs
were appointed by the governor.[7] During the greater part
of the eighteenth century, it was the custom for the court
of each county every year to recommend three of its justices
as suitable persons for the sheriffalty, one of whom the
governor would appoint sheriff for a term of one year.
The first of the three justices was often, if not usually,
selected by the governor, and so the power of choosing
sheriffs was by this custom practically placed in the hands
of the county courts.[8] The sheriff did not sit as a judge
in the county court, but he became a justice again after his
term had expired.[9] Sheriffs were appointed for only one
year; but during a considerable part of the colonial period,
their commissions could be renewed by the governor for a
second term.[10]

According to an account of Virginia written at the end
of the seventeenth century, the place of sheriff was a lucra-
tive one and was much sought after.[11] But by the end of the
first decade of the next century the tobacco currency had
fallen so low that it had become difficult to get suitable
persons to accept the sheriffalty. This refusal on the part
of the justices to serve when appointed sheriff led the as-

---

[6] Hening, II, 21, 78, 353. York County Records, 1671-1694, 26.

[7] These appointments were sometimes, and probably generally,
made with the advice of the council. Council Journal, 1721-1734,
285, 286, 289, 331, 332.

[8] Hartwell, Blair, and Chilton, 27, 28. Calendar Virginia State
Papers, I, 98, 99, 198. Hening, III, 246, 247; V, 515, 516. Webb,
Virginia Justice, 299. Starke, Virginia Justice, 325. Henrico Records, 1710-1714, 55, 79, 123, 154, 230; ibid., 1719-1724, 244, 264, 322;
ibid., 1737-1746, 297, 312. Warwick Records, 1748-1762, 11, 25, 137,
179.

[9] Webb, Virginia Justice, 293.

[10] Hening, I, 259, 442; II, 247; III, 246, 247; V, 515, 516; VII,
644. Robinson MSS., 451. Va. Mag. Hist. and Biog., II, 387, 388.

[11] Hartwell, Blair, and Chilton, 27, 28.

sembly to pass a law in 1710 which imposed a heavy fine on any one who should refuse the office when elected to it.[12]

Sheriffs in Virginia performed many of the same duties that they did in England, but they did not have power to hold courts as in the mother country. They executed the orders and sentences of the courts and the assembly, made arrests, summoned jurors and others to court. They also sometimes took the lists of tithables and usually collected the taxes.[13] In the early years sheriffs were wont to attend public meetings for the purpose of making arrests and serving warrants. The fear of meeting this officer caused many people to absent themselves from musters and from church on Sundays. This falling off of the attendance at these places not only affected the spiritual welfare of the people, but also hindered the transaction of public and private business. The assembly realized that this obstacle in the way of public meeting should be removed, and so in 1658 enacted that no warrants should thereafter be served on any one on the Sabbath or on muster days.[14] By subsequent statutes it was provided that no arrests except for felony, riots, and suspicion of treason, were to be made on Sundays, certain holidays, and muster and election days, and that no persons except residents of the town were to be arrested in James City during the period beginning five days before and ending five days after the meetings of the General Court and the assembly. Witnesses were also granted exemption from arrests except at the King's suit while attending the county or other courts and also while coming to and returning from the same. Councillors and sheriffs were privileged from arrest for debt and trespass while attending and going to and returning from the General Court and council meetings.[15]

---

[12] Spottswood's Letters, I, 56. Council Journal. 1721-1734, 54. Hening, III, 500, 501; IV, 84. Webb, Virginia Justice, 299.

[13] Hening, I, 333, 452, 465; II, 19, 83, 412; III, 264; VI, 247, 523, 566; VIII, 181. Winder MSS., I, 203, 204. Hartwell. Blair. and Chilton, 51. Webb, Virginia Justice, 293-295, 303. Chitty's Blackstone, I, pp. 252-254. Beverley, History of Virginia, Book IV, p. 13.

[14] Hening, I, 457.

[15] Hening, II, 86, 213, 502, 503. Webb, Virginia Justice, 15. Starke, Virginia Justice, 15.

In each county there was a jail, in which were detained offenders who had been sentenced to imprisonment by the county court and those criminals who were waiting to be sent to the public jail at Jamestown or Williamsburg. During the first part of the colonial period, criminals who were to be tried by the Quarter Court or the assembly were kept in the county jails while awaiting their trials. On the first day of every term of the Quarter Court or the assembly the sheriff of each county delivered the criminals that were in his custody to the sheriff of James City, who brought them before the governor and council or the assembly for trial.[16] But by the beginning of the eighteenth century (1705), it had become the custom to send criminals charged with offenses cognizable in the superior courts to the public jail at Williamsburg immediately after they had been given a preliminary hearing before the courts of examination in the counties.[17] Prisoners for debt, as well as criminals, were confined in the public jail at the capital. In 1724, there were two public prisons at Williamsburg; one for debtors, and another for criminals.[18] By a law of 1746 both classes of prisoners were to be kept in the same building, but one part of the prison was to be occupied by debtors and the other by criminals.[19]

The keeper of the prison in each county was the sheriff, who had to answer for all escapes due to his own negligence, but the commissioners were held responsible for those that were permitted by the insecurity of the prison-houses. Owing to the poverty of the counties, they did not in the early years have strong jails, and escapes from them were frequently made. The responsibility for these bore heavily on the sheriffs and commissioners, and the assembly declared, in a law passed in 1647 and re-enacted in 1658 and 1662, that any prison that was as strong as an average Vir-

---

[16] Hening, I, 264, 265, 398, 444.
[17] Hening, III, 390.
[18] Hugh Jones, Present State of Virginia, 30.
[19] Hening, VI, 135.

ginia house, and from which an escape could not be effected
without breaking through some part of the building, should
be deemed sufficiently secure. Persons breaking out of such
a house on being retaken were to be adjudged felons, and
the sheriffs and commissioners were not to be answerable for
jail-breakings in such cases.[20] Prison rules were in one respect more humane than they are at present. The prisoners
were not all shut off from the advantages of fresh air and
exercise, but most of them were allowed to walk about during the daytime within a certain area around the .jail. The
limits within which prisoners were allowed their freedom
were marked out by the justices, and by an act of 1765 were
to include an area of not less than five nor more than ten
acres. All prisoners except those charged with felony or
treason [21] who would give bond not to escape were allowed
the freedom of the prison grounds. But if any one abused
this privilege by going outside of the prescribed limits, he
was deprived of this liberty. The leniency of these regulations enabled some of the prisoners to reduce the punishment
of confinement almost to a minimum. Many persons sent to
jail for debt took houses within the prison limits, and thus
lived at home while serving out their terms of imprisonment. But the assembly did not intend that debtors should
get off with a nominal punishment, and so in 1661 passed a
law by which persons living within the limits of a prison
were not to be allowed to lodge in their own houses or be
permitted to walk over the grounds, but were to be kept
in close confinement.[22]

The laws providing for the payment of prison fees varied
from time to time. It was often required that the prisoner
himself pay the cost of his maintenance while in prison. By
laws enacted in 1711 and 1748, it was provided that prisoners

---

[20] Accomac Records, 1640-1645, 108, 201, 264, 270. Hening, I, 265,
340, 341, 452, 460; II, 77.

[21] By a law passed in 1662 this exception was also made against
persons under execution for debt. Hening, II, 77.

[22] Hening, I, 341; II, 19, 77; III, 15, 268; VIII, 119, 120. Warwick County Court Records, 1748-1762, 208, 340.

for debt were to have an allowance from the assembly if they were not able to pay their prison fees. Other statutes of this century placed upon creditors the burden of defraying the charges incurred in keeping insolvent debtors in prison.[23]

In colonial times, as well as at the present, the constables shared with the sheriff in the performance of the executive duties of the counties. We cannot say exactly when constables were first appointed, but we know that by 1637 the office had become an established part of the governmental machinery of the counties.[24] Constables were usually appointed by the county courts, though the first ones were chosen by the assembly.[25] Every county was divided into precincts, in each of which a constable was elected every year by the county court. Any person elected constable could be forced to accept the office, though he could be relieved from serving at the end of one year.[26] Many of the duties performed by the constable were the same as those discharged by the same officer in England, and were about the same as those that have engaged his successors in Virginia up to the present time.

Not only did he have to execute orders and decrees of the courts and the assembly, but he was also a conservator of the peace and had to arrest all those who were guilty of riotous and disorderly conduct. He was enjoined to " keep a watchful eye over the drinking and victualling houses and such persons as unlawfully frequent " such places. On him also devolved the duty of seeing that each farmer planted as many acres in corn as the law required, and did not allow suckers to grow after his tobacco had been cut.[27]

---

[23] Hening, I, 285, 449; IV, 27, 490; VI, 136; VIII, 527-529. Accomac Records, 1632-1640, 129; ibid., 1640-1645, 264.

[24] Accomac Records, 1632-1640, 69.

[25] Winder MSS., I, 129. York Records, 1671-1694, 72, 186, 235, 257. Essex Records, 1683-1686, 86. Elizabeth City County Records, 1684-1699, 18, 119. Henrico Records, 1710-1714, 42, 240; ibid., 1737-1746, 160, 191. Beverley, History of Virginia, Book IV, pp. 9, 14.

[26] Webb, Virginia Justice, 93.

[27] Accomac Records, 1640-1645, 82. Warwick Records, 1748-1762, 317. Webb, Virginia Justice, 90-95. Starke, Virginia Justice, 103-104. Hening, I, 246, 344. Chitty's Blackstone, I, pp. 264-265.

Constables took the leading part in the hue and cry. Whenever a robbery or murder was committed, the person robbed or any one else who was present could go to the nearest constable and " require him to raise the hue and cry to pursue the offender." Upon receiving such notice, the constable was to call on all the men of his precinct to assist him in his search for the felon. If they failed to find him in that precinct, the constable was to notify the constable of the next precint, and he the next, and so on until the offender " was apprehended or pursued to the seaside." The hue and cry could be raised by a constable without an order from a magistrate, but it was usually not done without a warrant from a justice.[28] The hue and cry could also be raised to pursue runaway slaves and servants.[29]

Another important office was that of clerk of the county court. County clerks were usually appointed by the secretary of state, and were regarded as his deputies. The appointments were not made for any definite period, but were revocable at the pleasure of the secretary.[30] This patronage not only extended the influence of the secretary throughout the colony, but also proved a source of considerable revenue to him, as it was the custom for all the clerks to pay him a fee every year. In 1700 these fees annually amounted to 36,200 pounds of tobacco.[31] In 1718, a bill was offered in the assembly providing that the power of appointing and removing clerks should be taken from the secretary and given to the justices of the peace. The reasons given by the advocates of the measure for the proposed changed in the

---

[28] Webb, Virginia Justice, 181.　Starke, Virginia Justice, 206, 207.
[29] Hening, I, 483; II, 299.
[30] In one of Bacon's laws it was provided that county clerks should be elected by the county courts. From the Accomac and Henrico court records we find that clerks were occasionally commissioned by the governor. But these exceptions to the usual method of choosing clerks seem not to have remained in force very long. Hening, II, 355. Accomac Records, 1640-1645, 146. Henrico Records, 1719-1724, 58; ibid., 1710-1714, 201; ibid., 1737-1746, 191. Sainsbury MSS., 1705-1707, 394, 408.
[31] Sainsbury, 1720-1730, 268. Va. Mag. of Hist. and Biog., VIII, 184.

method of choosing county clerks was that these clerks were often elected Burgesses, and as long as they held office at the pleasure of the secretary, an appointee of the king, the assembly would be too much under the influence of the governor. Governor Spottswood rightly considered the bill an attack on the King's prerogative, and declared his intention of vetoing it if it passed the assembly. The measure, therefore, failed, and county clerks continued to be appointed as before.[32]

The General Court and the oyer and terminer courts were served by the sheriffs of the county or counties in which the capital was located. According to Hartwell, Blair, and Chilton, the secretary of state was nominally the clerk of the General Court, and drew the salary that went with the place; but the duties of the office were performed by a deputy, who was styled clerk of the General Court, with the assistance of one or more under clerks. The place of secretary was one of the oldest and most important offices in the colony, and, as we have just seen, was considered of sufficient dignity to be filled by a direct commission from the King. In the office of the secretary, were kept the proceedings of the General Court and also a record of all probates and administrations, certificates of birth, marriage licenses, and the fines imposed by the county courts.[33]

Prior to 1662, there was not a notary public in Virginia. Owing to the lack of such an officer to attest oaths, statements sworn to in Virginia were not given the credit in foreign countries to which they were entitled. For this reason the assembly in 1662 appointed one notary public for the colony, and some years later authorized him to choose deputies throughout the colony.[34]

Lawyers are seldom alluded to in the early county court records,[35] though frequent mention is made of attorneys.

[32] Spottswood's Letters, II, 279.
[33] Beverley, History of Virginia, Book IV, pp. 10-11. Hartwell, Blair, and Chilton, 48-51.
[34] Hening, II, 136, 316, 456, 457.
[35] York Records, 1633-1694, 11.

But these attorneys were not always lawyers. A person living in one county and owning property in another frequently appointed an attorney to represent him in the county in which his property was situated. These powers of attorney, as well as notices of the termination of the legal agency created by them, were recorded in the proceedings of the county courts.[36] Though the lawyers in the earliest years were few in number, yet by 1643 they had become important enough to call forth special legislation for their profession. In this year it was provided by an act of assembly that lawyers should not be allowed to practice in any court until after they had been licensed in the Quarter Court. They were also restricted in their charges to twenty pounds of tobacco for every cause pleaded in the monthly courts and to fifty pounds for every one in the Quarter Court. Besides no case could be refused by any lawyer unless he had already been employed on the other side.[37] Within two years the assembly repented of having allowed lawyers this small amount of liberty, and it passed a law prohibiting attorneys from practicing in the courts for money. The reason given by the assembly for this action was that suits had been unnecessarily multiplied by the " unskillfullness and covetousness of attorneys." [38] The exclusion of lawyers from the courts must have worked a hardship on those parties to suits who were intellectually inferior to their opponents, and it soon became necessary to modify this statute. A less stringent law against attorneys was passed two years later, though by it compensation was still denied professional lawyers. By this act it was provided that whenever a court perceived that a litigant would suffer injustice because of his inability to cope with his opponent, the court was either to open the cause itself or else " appoint some fitt man out of

---

[36] Accomac Records, 1632-1640, 57, 161, 162. York Records, 1633-1694, 118, 151, 185, 202. Essex Records, 1683-1686, 60. Henrico Records, 1677-1692, 160, 167.
[37] This act did not apply to special attorneys or those that had letters of procuration from England. Hening, I, 275, 276.
[38] Ibid., I, 302.

the people to plead the cause, and allow him satisfaction requisite." [39] By 1656, the assembly had come to realize the inconvenience attendant upon the administration of justice without the assistance of lawyers, and this time voted a repeal of all the laws against " mercenary attorneys." [40] But professional attorneys were given only a short lease of life by this act of repeal. In 1658, it was enacted that any one receiving pay for pleading in any case in any court in the colony should be fined 5000 pounds of tobacco. Every one that pleaded as an attorney for another had to take an oath that he would take no compensation either directly or indirectly for his services. At this time the question was raised by the governor and council whether this law was not a violation of Magna Charta. But the Burgesses saw nothing in the measure that was contrary to the principles of that document, and it became a law despite the doubt as to its constitutionality. [41] The courts must have gotten along badly without the assistance of paid attorneys; for in 1680 the assembly again passed a law which recognized the right of lawyers to charge for their services. This same statute also provided that no attorney-at-law should plead in any court until after he had been licensed by the governor. The reason given by the assembly for imposing this restriction on the practice of the law was that the courts had been annoyed by ignorant and impertinent persons pleading in the interest of their friends. These volunteer attorneys sometimes pleaded for parties to suits without being asked to do so by them, and often did injury to the causes advocated by them. [42] The law of 1680 was soon afterwards repealed, but professional attorneys had been again admitted to the courts by 1718. During the eighteenth century we find no statutes forbidding lawyers to receive compensation for their services, but the fees charged by them continued to be restricted

---

[39] Hening, I, 349.
[40] Hening, I, 419.
[41] Hening, I, 482, 483, 495, 496.
[42] Hening, II, 478, 479.

by the assembly. By the laws of 1680 and 1718, lawyers'
fees were fixed at fifty shillings, or 500 pounds of tobacco,
for every cause pleaded in the General Court and fifteen shillings, or 150 pounds of tobacco, for every one in the county
courts.[43]

It is not easy to explain this opposition of the assembly to
the legal profession. Mr. John B. Minor thought that it
had its origin in the jealousy between the aristocracy of
birth represented by the assembly and the aristocracy of
merit represented by the lawyers.[44] It is more probable that
this unfriendly attitude of the ruling class towards the legal
fraternity was caused by the lack of ability and character of
the early lawyers. Attorneys' fees, even when allowed to be
charged, were fixed so low by law that little encouragement
was given to men of ability to qualify themselves properly
for the profession. It is not unlikely, therefore, that during
the greater part of the seventeenth century the attempts at
pleading made by many of the lawyers were a hindrance to
the proper administration of justice, and if so, the prejudice
of the assembly against " mercenary attorneys " was not
without foundation. This feeling of hostility to lawyers
still finds its counterpart in the present-day belief of many
people, especially in the backward districts, that the duties
of the legal profession are incompatible with high moral
rectitude.

While professional lawyers were not excluded from the
courts by the.laws passed in the eighteenth century, yet the
courts were, for a considerable part of this century, closed to
those would-be lawyers who had not been properly licensed.
It has just been shown that the statutes of 1643 and 1680
provided for the licensing of attorneys by the governor or
Quarter Court. Similar provisions are found in laws
enacted in the eighteenth century. According to a law

---

[43] Hening, II, 479, 498; IV, 59; VI, 371-372. Sainsbury MSS.,
1640-1691, 215, 324. Randolph MSS., 444. Mercer, Virginia Laws,
19, 20. Beverley, History of Virginia, Book IV, p. 24.
[44] Minor's Institutes, 1st ed., Vol. IV, Part I, pp. 163-168.

passed in 1732, the governor and council were to receive all applications for licenses to practice in the inferior courts, and were to refer them to such persons, learned in the law, as they should see fit to select, who were to examine the candidates and report to the governor and council as to their qualifications. Upon the receipt of this report, the governor and council were to license such of the candidates as had proved themselves qualified to enter upon the profession and were to reject the others. The governor and council could also, for just cause, suspend any lawyer from practicing in the inferior courts. If a practitioner in an inferior court should at any time be neglectful of his duty, he was to pay all the damage occasioned by such neglect. But the provisions of this act did not extend to lawyers practicing in the General Court or to " any counsellor or barrister at law whatsoever." [45] This law was repealed in 1742, but another was passed in 1745, which contained about the same provision for the licensing of attorneys except that it required the governor and council to select only councillors as examiners of applicants for licenses. [46]

It does not appear whether the government ever entirely recovered from its early prejudice against professional attorneys; but from an order made by the court of Augusta County in 1746, it would seem that the justices of that region were still of the belief that the conduct of lawyers in court sometimes became a nuisance. The following order was made by the court in February of that year: " That any attorney interrupting another at the bar, or speaking when he is not employed, forfeit five shillings." [47] Apparently, the General Court also regarded the much-speaking of the lawyers as a nuisance, as the assembly felt called upon to pass a law in 1748 forbidding more than two lawyers on a side to plead in the General Court except in cases of life and death. [48]

---

[45] Hening, IV, 360-362.
[46] Ibid., V, 171, 345; VI, 140-143, 371-372.
[47] Virginia Historical Register, Vol. II, No. I, p. 15.
[48] Hening, VI, 143.

During the first years of the colony's history, there was no attorney-general in Virginia to give legal advice to the Quarter Court. But the governor and council could send to England for an opinion if a cause came before them involving a question of law which they felt incapable of deciding.⁴⁹ The first attorney-general mentioned in the records was Richard Lee, who was appointed in 1643.⁵⁰ It is not stated from whom Lee received his appointment; but the later attorneys-general were appointed by the governor, and sometimes with the consent of the King.⁵¹ Prior to 1703, the attorney-general was not required to live at the capital, but in that year the salary of the office was raised from forty to one hundred pounds sterling, and its incumbent was required to take up his residence in Williamsburg.⁵² The attorney-general had to prosecute criminals before the General Court and the oyer and terminer courts, and to give his advice to these courts whenever it was needed.⁵³

In 1711, it was found necessary to appoint prosecuting attorneys for the counties.⁵⁴ At that time breaches of the penal laws were prosecuted in the counties by those persons who had reported them to the courts, and informers were given one-half of all the fines imposed for offenses reported by them. It sometimes happened that the informer would compound with the accused for his half of the fines and would then stop the prosecution. This would cause the case to be thrown out of court, and, so the crown would fail to

⁴⁹ Sainsbury MSS., 1618-1624, 109-110.

⁵⁰ Va. Mag. of Hist. and Biog., VIII, 70.

⁵¹ Sainsbury MSS., 1625-1705, 66, 77; ibid., 1691-1697, 331; ibid., 1706-1714, 449. Virginia Gazette, Nov. 18, 1737.

⁵² The salary did not continue so high until the end of the period; in 1755 it was only seventy pounds sterling. Sainsbury, 1625-1705, 30, 59, 61, 66, 77. Dinwiddie Papers, I, 390.

⁵³ Calendar Virginia State Papers, I, 94, 100, 161. General Court Records, 1670-1676, 116. Randolph MSS., 432. MSS. in Va. Histor. Soc., 23, 24. Webb, Virginia Justice, 113.

⁵⁴ But before this time, as early as 1665, we find mention of a prosecuting attorney for Accomac County. This officer was perhaps a prosecuting attorney specially appointed for Accomac County because of its isolation and distance from Williamsburg. Neill, Virginia Carolorum, 315.

receive its half of the fine. There was need, therefore, of a better method of prosecuting offenders in the counties, and Governor Spottswood, following a recommendation of the attorney-general, issued a proclamation appointing prosecuting attorneys for the counties.[55] These new officers came to stay, and from this time on we find them performing their duties in the county courts. They were deputies of the attorney-general and had to prosecute offenders in the county courts as the attorney-general did in the General Court and oyer and terminer courts. They were also required to see that all the fines imposed by the county courts were reported to the secretary's office to be recorded.

---

[55] Hening, IV, 545, 546.
[56] Henrico Records, 1710-1714, 193; ibid., 1719-1724, 337; ibid., 1737-1746, 360. Warwick Records, 1748-1762, 162, 324, 373.

CONCLUSIONS.

From the facts presented in this study, the following conclusions may be drawn:

(1) The judiciary was in all its branches closely allied to the other departments of the government. Prior to 1682, the legislature was the highest court of appeal in the colony, and it was closely connected with both the superior and inferior courts during the entire colonial period. The judges of the General Court constituted the upper house of the assembly, and the justices of the county courts were often elected to seats in the lower house. Besides, the judges of the General Court, as members of the governor's council, performed executive duties for the colony at large, and the justices of the county courts performed administrative duties in their respective counties.

(2) The authority of the judiciary was subordinate to that of the legislature. No law enacted by the assembly could be declared unconstitutional and set aside by the courts.

(3) The judiciary was aristocratic in its organization, and from 1682 to the Revolution the people had no voice, either direct or indirect, in the choice of their judges. Even prior to 1682, the assembly was the only court in which the judges were elected directly by the people. During the Commonwealth period, the judges of the General Court were chosen by the representatives of the people, and for a short while during this period justices of the county courts were appointed with the consent of the assembly. But with these exceptions, the colonial judiciary was thoroughly aristocratic in all its branches.

(4) The position of judge in both the superior and inferior courts was one of honor and dignity, and was usually held by men of ability. The judges of the General Court

were very influential in the colony, and were often able to curb the power of the governor. Their opposition to the King's representative probably contributed much towards keeping the colony from falling into a state of close dependence upon the crown. It is also not improbable that out of this opposition to the governor there grew up that spirit of resistance to the crown which both the aristocracy and the people showed in the Revolutionary period.

(5) The courts were bound in their decisions by the common law of England, the Parliamentary statutes passed prior to 1607, and by the statutes enacted by the Virginia Assembly. But a legal education was not a requisite qualification for judges, and apparently many, if not most, of the judges both of the superior and inferior courts, came to the bench without special legal training. Therefore, in arriving at decisions, they frequently had to rely, especially in the early years, on their own judgment for guidance more than on law and precedents.

(6) Each county had a court which met at regular intervals and the justices of the peace exercised certain judicial powers out of court. As these magistrates lived in different parts of the county, justice was thus brought almost to the doors of the people. In the documents that have been examined very few complaints against the inferior courts are recorded, and it seems that these tribunals as a rule administered justice fairly and impartially.

(7) There were certain latent weaknesses in the constitution of the General Court which occasionally gave rise to abuses in actual practice. But as only a few cases of such abuses have been found, it may safely be inferred that justice was as a rule fairly administered by the superior, as well as the inferior, courts.

MANUSCRIPTS.

(A complete bibliography is not attempted, but only those manuscript sources are mentioned to which reference has been made. The titles of the printed materials are given with sufficient fulness in the footnotes.)

Accomac County Court Records (1632-1645). 2 v. State Library, Richmond, Va.

Charles City County Court Records (1758-1762). Virginia Historical Society, Richmond, Va.

Collingwood, Edward, MSS. 2 v. Folio. Library of Congress, Washington, D. C.

Council Journal (1721-1734). State Library, Richmond, Va.

De Jarnette MSS. 2 v. Folio. State Library, Richmond, Va.

Elizabeth City County Court Records (1684-1699). State Library, Richmond, Va.

Essex County Court Records (1683-1699). 2 v. State Library, Richmond, Va.

Henrico County Court Records (1677-1746). 4 v. Henrico Courthouse and State Library, Richmond, Va.

Journal of the Virginia Assembly (1697-1720). State Library, Richmond, Va.

Lower Norfolk County Court Records (1637-1643). Virginia Historical Society.

Ludwell MSS. 5 v. Virginia Historical Society, Richmond, Va.

McDonald, Col. Angus M. MSS. relating to the early history of Virginia. 5 v. State Library, Richmond, Va.

Randolph, John, of Roanoke, MSS. Virginia Historical Society.

Rappahannock County Court Records (1686-1692). State Library, Richmond, Va.

Records of the General Court of Virginia (1670-1676). Virginia Historical Society.

Richmond County Court Records. State Library, Richmond, Va.

Robinson, Conway, MSS. Abstracts of General Court Records and other valuable papers since destroyed. Virginia Historical Society.

Sainsbury MSS. copied from the British Public Record Office. 20 v. Folio. State Library, Richmond, Va.

Surry County Court Records (1645-1672). State Library, Richmond, Va.

Virginia Court Book (1623-1626). A record of the early judicial proceedings of the Governor and Council of Virginia. Library of Congress, Washington, D. C.

Warwick County Court Records (1748-1762). State Library, Richmond, Va.

Winder MSS. Copies from British Public Record Office. State Library, Richmond, Va.

York County Court Records (1633-1694). 2 v. State Library, Richmond, Va.